WOMAN'S PROFESSION AS MOTHER AND EDUCATOR, WITH VIEWS IN OPPOSITION TO WOMAN SUFFRAGE

First published 1872
This edition published by Lector House in 2024

ISBN: 978-93-6138-465-3

Lector House LLP
Registered Office: H. No. 96, Block C, Tomar Colony,
Burari, Delhi – 110084, India
info@lectorhouse.com
www.lectorhouse.com

WOMAN'S PROFESSION AS MOTHER AND EDUCATOR, WITH VIEWS IN OPPOSITION TO WOMAN SUFFRAGE

CATHARINE ESTHER BEECHER

2024

LECTOR HOUSE

LECTOR HOUSE LLP

WOMAN'S PROFESSION AS MOTHER AND EDUCATOR, WITH VIEWS IN OPPOSITION TO WOMAN SUFFRAGE

BY

CATHARINE E. BEECHER

Dedication.

To the Ministers of Religion in the United States.

Fathers and Brethren:

As the daughter and sister of nine ministers of Jesus Christ you will allow me to address you by those endeared names; and also because there is an emergency that demands unusual measures.

This *woman movement* is one which is uniting by co-operating influences, all the antagonisms that are warring on the family state. Spiritualism, free-love, free divorce, the vicious indulgences consequent on unregulated civilization, the worldliness which tempts men and women to avoid *large* families, often by sinful methods, thus making the ignorant masses the chief supply of the future ruling majorities; and most powerful of all, the feeble constitution and poor health of women, causing them to dread maternity as—what it is fast becoming—an accumulation of mental and bodily tortures.

Add to this, that extreme fastidiousness which not only excludes needful instruction from the pulpit, but makes mothers shrink from learning and teaching those dangers which their daughters most need to know, and prevents medical men and even women physicians from uttering needful warnings.

I once said to a lady physician with an enormous practice, in reply to some of her statements, "why do you not call the mothers of this city together and tell them all this?" She replied "it is impossible—they would not hear me—I should have to nail the doors and windows to keep them—and if they did hear, they would not believe."

It is the *women teachers of our common schools* who must be instructed to become lecturers on health in all our school districts and teach mothers how to instruct children in all the laws of health and the dreadful penalties which in certain directions are but little known and now threaten the ruin of the rising generation. There is no duty more difficult than this; for it is one which if done properly saves from danger, and if improperly leads to it.

If the clergy of this nation will give their powerful influence to promote the aims of this work in modes they will more wisely devise than I can suggest, success will be ensured; and to them I appeal (as I used to do to a beloved father and as I often do to dear brothers,) to help me where my own strength and courage fail.

With christian love and respect,

Yours truly,

CATHARINE E. BEECHER.

Contents

Page

Introduction.

The object of the following pages is to present the subject of woman's profession as mother and chief educator of our race in connection with the present demand that she shall also assume the responsibilities of civil government.

However great or small may be the probabilities as to the imposition of woman suffrage, it is certain that there is just cause for alarm at organizations all over the land sending out women of talents and benevolence to lecture, and scattering tracts and newspapers by hundreds of thousands, advocating principles and measures destructive both to the purity and the perpetuity of the family state.

This little volume consists of *unpublished* addresses—all but the first—to meetings of ladies only, and its design is to meet the false principles and false reasonings on the subject of "woman's rights" now working extensive evils that are little realized.

It is offered with the deep conviction that an important crisis in our national history is impending, and that it is the intelligent and conscientious women of our country who eventually will decide whether the result shall be beneficial or most disastrous.

An Address on Female Suffrage,

Delivered in the Music Hall of Boston, in December, 1870.

I appear this evening to present the views of that large portion of my sex who are opposed to such a change of our laws and customs as would place the responsibility of civil government on woman.

This may be done without impugning the motives, or the character, or the measures of that respectable party who hold the contrary position. As in the physical universe the nicely-balanced *centripetal* and *centrifugal* forces hold in steady curve every brilliant orbit, so, in the moral world, the radical element, which would forsake the beaten path of ages, is held in safe and steady course by the conservative; while that, also, is preserved from dangerous torpor by the antagonistic power.

And so, while claiming to represent the conservative element, I meet with respect and kindness my centrifugal friend.

First, let me state the points in which we agree, that we may more clearly appreciate those in which we differ.

We agree, then, on the general principle, that woman's happiness and usefulness are equal in value to those of man's, and, consequently, that she has a right to equal advantages for securing them.

We agree, also, that woman, even in our own age and country, has never been allowed such equal advantages, and that multiplied wrongs and suffering have resulted from this injustice.

Finally, we agree that it is the right and the duty of every woman to employ the power of organization and agitation, in order to gain those advantages which are given to the one sex, and unjustly withheld from the other.

My object, in this address, is not to discuss the question of woman's natural and abstract right to the ballot, nor to point out the evils that might follow the exercise of this power, nor to controvert the opinions of those advocating woman's suffrage in any particular point.

Instead of this, I propose, first, to present reasons for assuming that it must be a very long time before woman suffrage can be gained; so that the evils it is hoped to cure by the ballot would continue and increase for a long period; and, secondly, to present another method for gaining the advantages unjustly withheld; and thus to remedy wrongs which both parties are seeking to redress.

The first reason for believing that the gift of the ballot must be long delayed is, that it is contrary to the customs of Christian people, by which the cares of civil life, and the outdoor and heavy labor which take a man from home, are given to the stronger sex, and the lighter labor and care of the family state, to woman.

The more society has advanced in civilization and in Christian culture, the more perfectly have these *distinctive* divisions of responsibility for the two sexes been maintained; and in no age or country more strictly than in our own.

Those of us who oppose woman suffrage concede that there are occasions in which general laws and customs should yield to temporary emergencies; as when, in the stress of family sickness, the husband becomes nurse and cook; or, in the extremities of war, the women plow, sow, and reap; and it were well if every boy and girl were so trained that they could wisely meet such emergencies.

But while this is conceded, the main question is still open, namely, Is there any such emergency in our national history as demands so great a change in our laws and customs as would be involved in placing the responsibilities of civil government on our whole sex? For, with the gift of the ballot, comes the connected responsibility of framing wise laws to regulate finance, war, agriculture, commerce, mining, manufactures, and all the many fields of man's outdoor labor. And the charge of these outdoor responsibilities would be assigned by the ballot; and not alone to that class of women who are demanding woman suffrage, but *to our whole sex*.

For, whenever the time comes that a single vote of one woman may decide the most delicate, the most profound, and the most perilous measures of the state and nation, it will be the duty of every woman, not only to go to the polls, but to vote intelligently and conscientiously.

It is in view of such considerations that, at the present time, a large majority of American women would regard the gift of the ballot, not as a privilege conferred, but as an act of oppression, forcing them to assume responsibilities belonging to man, for which they are not and can not be qualified; and, consequently, withdrawing attention and interest from the distinctive and more important duties of their sex. For the question is not whether a class of women, who have no family responsibilities, shall take charge of civil government; but it is whether this duty shall be imposed on the whole of our sex. With the chivalrous tenderness toward woman so prevalent in our nation, this would never be done till at least a majority of women ask for it; and the time must be afar off ere such a majority will be found.

I wish to verify this statement by an extract from one of the many letters of sympathy and approbation received since it became known that I am publicly to present my views on Woman Suffrage:

> "MY DEAR MADAM: Though personally a stranger, I feel strongly impelled to write and thank you for coming before the public in opposition to the advocates of woman suffrage.
>
> "I have no doubt that an exceedingly large majority of the educated and thoughtful women of the country feel a strong personal repugnance to becoming voters, as well as a conviction that this proposed innovation, far from working a beneficial change in the condition of the country, would actually lower the present standard of political morality. But they form a class but little accustomed to make their voices heard outside of their own social circle, and therefore in danger of being overlooked by those reformers who, with a thankworthy zeal for 'woman's rights,' are, as I think, striving to perpetrate a great *woman's wrong*.
>
> "It is sometimes said that all women ought at least to have a chance to vote, if they wish it; but none are obliged to do so unless they like. And when compliant men have said this, they consider themselves magnanimous and chivalrous, and think the whole question happily settled.
>
> "It might be so if we had *no conscience*. But wider privileges mean wider duties. From the bottom of my soul I hate the idea of meeting women at the polls; and yet, if woman suffrage ever becomes a fact, I can not stay away. For my fraction of power inevitably makes me thus much responsible for the civil government of my country. If I *may* vote, I *must* vote. I have no right, by withholding my vote, to throw its weight into the wrong scale. And yet, held back as I am, and must be, from the life of the street, the caucus, and the primary political meetings, and not more by my incapacity for man's work than by his incapacity for mine—living chiefly at home, because my work is home work—what can I know of the fitness of candidates for local offices, or of the machinery of political parties?"

This perspicuous statement expresses the present views of probably nine tenths of the most intelligent and conscientious women of our country. Were it the question whether the responsibilities of civil government should be assumed by this class of women alone, the risks of an affirmative decision would be small. But let us consider the other classes that would be included in universal woman suffrage.

Next to the more intelligent class represented by this letter-writer, would come a large body of those whose generous *impulses* take the lead, rather than the cool deductions of reason and experience.

It is this class of enthusiasts that would most confidently attempt to conduct the affairs of the state.

Next to these would come the great body of busy and easy women, who, from pliant kindness and confidence, would vote as fathers, brothers, and husbands advised.

Next to these most respectable classes would come the superficial, the unreflecting, and the frolicsome, to serve only as tools for political wire-pullers.

Then would come the lovers of notoriety, the ambitious—the lovers of power—the caterers for public offices, and the seekers for money. Of these, the most unprincipled would employ the distinctive power of their sex in caucuses, in jury-boxes, and in legislative and congressional committees; thus adding another to the many deteriorating influences of political life.

Next would come that vast mass of ignorant women whose consciences and votes would be controlled by a foreign and domestic priesthood.

Lastly would come the most degraded and despised, who would like nothing better than to insult and oppose those who look down upon them with disgust and contempt.

Lead all these classes to the polls, and the result would be a vast increase of the incompetent and dangerous voters. It would, to a still greater extent, place the wealth and intelligence of the nation under those without intelligence, who, for their own advantage, would lavish wealth on useless schemes, and vote away the property of the industrious to support the indolent and vicious. In many of our large cities we are witnessing the beginning of this impending danger.

Still another reason for such a conclusion is the fact that, though the Woman's Suffrage party at present is increasing in numbers, the discussion it has produced is gradually changing the views of many sensible persons who at first were its advocates. That has been the case with myself. For, on the first consideration of the matter, it seemed right and proper that women should have a voice in deciding who should be their rulers and make their laws; and that the simple dropping a vote into the ballot-box could be done without risk to womanly delicacy, and without danger of any kind. This was before discussion had revealed the more comprehensive bearings of the question, which finally removed me, as it has many others, to the opposite side of the question.

If, then, agitation increases the party seeking the ballot, and yet discussion is constantly withdrawing large numbers of the more intelligent and reflective, the time must be far distant when woman suffrage will be secured.

Another reason for believing that woman suffrage is afar off is the character of the men who appear to favor this change of our political status, and also their modes of meeting the question. The estimate of women by the other sex depends very greatly on the character of the mothers, wives, and sisters with whom they have associated, or on the character of the female society they most frequent. Those who associate with superficial, weak, or unprincipled women, form a low opinion of the whole sex which is false and unjust. On the contrary, those associated with the highest class of women place a halo of purity, strength, and honor on the brow of the whole sex, which is equally exaggerated. It is this last class of men who are foremost advocates of woman suffrage, and their estimate of woman's ability to manage civil government is to be taken with considerable though honorable deductions.

Another class of amiable, unreflecting men, having had a chivalrous training, are ready to give the "dear creatures" any thing they will please to ask.

Still another class of kind-hearted men say, "Yes, oh! yes, let them have the ballot and all the duties it involves, and they soon will wish to relinquish such responsibilities."

Then there are the political wire-pullers, who perceive that by catering to this, which they secretly deem a folly, they can make it subserve their selfish plans.

Lastly, there is a large number of intelligent and patriotic men who have not, as yet, so investigated the probable results of so fundamental a change in civil matters as to feel prepared to make any practical decision on the question, and so they give no decided answers.

These several classes of amiable and intelligent men are those who finally will decide the question, and they are the last who would force the responsibilities of the civil state on an unwilling minority of our sex; much less would they force it on a majority who would regard it as an unjust and unchivalrous exercise of power. For this reason it seems almost certain that the ballot will not be given to American women till it is clear that a majority are willing to take such responsibilities; and the time when this assurance can be gained must be at a very remote period.

Another reason for this conclusion is the powerful influences at the command of those of my sex who are opposed to this measure. Multitudes of women are now quiet and silent because they have little fear of danger in this direction. But should a time come when the woman suffrage party seem near achieving their aim, there would be measures instituted the power of which, as yet, is little known or appreciated. For *they too* would organize all over the nation and summon to their aid both the pulpit and the press. All the Catholic clergy, to a man, would lend their influence against a measure so contrary to the tenets and spirit of a church that enforces subordination and obedience as prime virtues. Not less decided would be the influence of all the Jewish rabbis.

The Protestant clergy, who have ever been like their Master, the sympathizing friends of woman, would be the last to enforce new and heavy responsibilities on our sex, contrary to the wishes even of a small, intelligent, and conscientious minority.

Not less decided are the great majority of the conductors of the press; and if an emergency calls for it, by the coöperation of such powerful auxiliaries, we could bring such an array of petitions and remonstrances in bulk and respectable names as never before entered congressional halls.

The attempt to force woman suffrage on us by making it a political question would also be met by a counter-influence that would convince every demagogue that any man or party which forces us to the polls will be ostracized by the votes of every woman who is thus dragged from her appropriate sphere to bear the burdens of the state.

Another and the final reason for believing female suffrage at a distant future is the proposed circuitous and indirect mode of remedying evils which could be relieved by a much more direct and speedy method. As things now are, men have the physical power that can force obedience; in most cases they have the power of the purse, and in all cases, they have the civil power. They can not be forced by the weaker sex to resign this power. It must be sought, then, as the gift of justice and benevolence. If, then, there are laws and customs that we deem unjust and oppressive, the short and common sense mode would be to petition the law-makers to change these laws according to the rules of justice and mercy. Instead of this the plea is, "We can not trust you to make laws; give us the ballot, and we will take better care of ourselves than you have done or will do." Now, any class of men who, after such an implication of their intelligence and justice, would give the ballot to woman, would most surely be those most ready to redress any wrongs for which the ballot is sought. Why should we not rather take the shorter and surer mode and *ask for the thing needed,* instead of the circuitous and uncertain mode involved in the ballot? Any man who would grant the ballot would grant all for which the ballot is sought.

As one proof of this, we have the changes which have been made in the laws of New-York State, as reported in a New-York paper. The agitation for women's rights commenced in that State, and now its laws give not only as many but more advantages to women than to men. For in that State, the wife has unlimited control of her own property, independently of her husband, while by law he must support her and her children. What is *his* is *hers,* but what is hers is *not* his. She may be rich and the husband poor, and yet he must pay all her debts. Her creditors can seize his property to pay her debts, but must leave hers untouched. He is obliged by law to support her; but however rich she may be, she is not obliged to support him. She may turn her husband out of the house she owns, but the law will not sustain the husband in such an act. The husband can not compel his wife to follow him if he changes residence. She may absent herself night and day, and, unless criminality is proved, the law gives no redress. At the same time, *divorce* is more easily obtained by a woman than a man.

With such an example before us, will it not be wisest to ask for such laws as we need before we seek the more uncertain ballot?

At the commencement of this discussion, it was stated that the parties at issue agree in these general principles, namely, that woman's usefulness and happiness are equal in value to man's, and consequently that she has a right to equal advantages for gaining them; that she is unjustly deprived of such equal advantages, and that organization and agitation to gain them is her privilege and duty.

The points of difference are as to the nature of the advantages of which she is deprived, the consequent evils, and the mode of remedy. One party regard woman's exclusion from the professions, the universities, and the civil offices of men as the leading injustice from which most of the evils complained of are the result, and that the gift of the ballot will prove the panacea for all these wrongs. The other party believe the chief cause of evils which both are striving to remedy is the want of a just appreciation of woman's profession, and the want of such a liberal and practical training for its duties as men secure for their most honored professions.

Here we again may refer to a patent maxim of common sense, which is this: that the more difficult and important are any duties, the more scientific care and training should be bestowed on those who are to perform them. It has been in obedience to this maxim that, in Christian countries, the highest advantages have been given to those men who have charge of the spiritual and eternal interests of our race. Most of the universities of Europe and of this country were founded to educate the clergy. Next came the training of those who administer laws, and then of those who cure the sick. These are named the *liberal professions,* because society has most liberally provided for the scientific training of those who perform these duties.

That women need as much and even more scientific and practical training for their appropriate business than men, arises from the fact that they must perform duties quite as difficult and important, and a much greater variety of them. A man usually selects one branch of business for a son, and, after his school education, secures an apprenticeship of years to perfect his practical skill; and thus a success is attained which would be impossible were he to practice various trades and professions.

Now let us notice the various and difficult duties that are demanded of woman in her ordinary relations as wife, mother, housekeeper, and the mistress of servants.

First, she has charge of the economies of the family state; for, as the general rule, men are to earn the support and women administer these earnings. In this must be included the style in which a house shall be prepared and furnished, so as best to secure pure air, sunlight, and the best arrangement and conveniences for labor. If women were scientifically trained in this particular, their influence would have saved much labor and much expense. But let the graduates of our female colleges be questioned as to the position and swing of doors to avoid draughts;

or of windows, to secure sunlight where most needed; or of chimneys, to secure ventilation and economize fuel; or on the most successful modes of ventilation; or on the most economical arrangement of closets, store-room, and pantry, to save time and steps; and it will be found, ordinarily, that nothing at all has been done to prepare them to answer intelligently such important practical questions.

There is no department of domestic economy where there is more enormous waste than in the selection and management of fuel. Much science is involved in learning what fuel is made of; what kinds best furnish warmth without waste; what methods waste heat; what methods preserve it; what spreads it equally; what creates draughts and thus colds and headaches, and many other connected subjects. Having devoted more than usual attention to this topic, and especially to the proper selection and management of furnaces and cook-stoves, it is my firm belief that if I could impart to the housekeepers of our country the knowledge I have gained, (and that without any help from scientific schools,) it would enable them to save millions of money and an enormous amount of ill health and discomfort.

Again, a housekeeper has charge of the selection and preparation of the food on which family health and enjoyment so much depend. To prepare her for this duty she should be taught what kinds of food are most healthful and nutritious; what kinds are best for the young and what for the aged; how each should be cooked to secure most nutriment and least waste; the relative value of buying wholesale or retail; the best modes of storing food and of preserving it from vermin or decay; what dishes are at once economical, comely, and inviting and how a husband's earnings can secure the most comfort and enjoyment with the most economical outlay. A woman needs training and instruction in this department of her duties as much as her sons need similar instruction and training in agriculture or watch-making, when that is to be their profession.

Again, the mistress of a family controls the selection and making of the clothing and furniture, and will be called to decide what is most suitable and economical; what stuffs wear longest; what hold colors best; what parts wear out soonest, and how they can be made to last the longest; how much is needed for each garment; and what is the proper way to cut and fit each article; what is the proper way of mending; what is the most economical and easiest mode of washing and ironing; and so on through a long list of duties that demand judgment, science, and care.

Again, the health of a family is especially a responsibility that rests upon woman. There is no such wise and needed physician as a well-instructed mother and housekeeper; not to cure—for that is the physician's part, but to prevent—disease, or stop it at the starting. Our gravest illnesses come from neglected colds, indigestion, and headaches.

Who first finds out when one is ill, and is best prepared to search for the cause? Why should not every housekeeper know the first symptoms of common illnesses, the cause and the cure? Not chiefly in the hospital or by the bedside is a well-instructed nurse needed, but by the family fireside, where she can observe the first symptoms, give early warning, and apply the simple cure. There is no technical training so valuable to a woman as that which enables her to keep the doctor out of the house, and to send for him when he is needed.

Again, to woman must be committed the charge of new-born infants—and of the mothers at the most perilous and most anxious period of life, and one demanding so much discretion, tenderness, and self-denying labor. Thousands of young, uninstructed mothers are sent out of life or made suffering invalids from their own ignorance of all they most need to know, or from the neglect or ignorance of untrained nurses.

The departments of practical life, to which the majority of women are ordained, ought to receive the honors and aid of lectures, professorships, endowments, and scientific treatment; the same as is bestowed to fit men for practical life. The care of a house, the conduct of a home, the management of children, the instruction and government of servants, are as deserving of scientific treatment and scientific professors and lectureships as are the care of farms, the management of manure and crops, and the raising and care of stock. Shall man secure for himself endowments, and professors, and lectures on stock-raising, the diseases of domestic animals, and the laws by which they are preserved in health, and woman be denied equal advantages for learning the laws by which health, beauty, and mental soundness may be secured to the more precious children under her care?

It is granted by all parties that it is women who are to nurse and train the children the first years of life, and they must do it either ignorantly and blunderingly, or intelligently guided by scientific knowledge. For this reason every college and high-school for women should have a well-instructed woman professor, whose duty it shall be to instruct young women (in the last years of their education) in all they need to know as wife, mother, nurse, and guardian of infancy and childhood.

For young men we find endowed scientific schools to teach them agricultural chemistry, that they may learn wisely to conduct a farm; why should not women be taught domestic chemistry and domestic philosophy? The more civilization advances, the more do complicated contrivances multiply for the charge of which women are mainly responsible. The laws that regulate heat, as applied in the construction of furnaces, stoves, ranges, and grates; the principles of hydraulics, as applied in constructing cisterns, boilers, water-pipes, faucets, and other multiplied modern conveniences, demand scientific and intelligent supervision impossible to a woman untrained in this department of her domestic duties.

Again, young men are provided with lectures on political economy, while domestic economy, as yet, has not been so honored. Most women come to the duty of providing for a family utterly ignorant of the science of comparative values, and of the greater or less economies of the articles they are to provide and preserve.

But the most important of all the departments of a woman's profession is one for which no college or high-school for women has made any proper provision.

Woman, as mother and as teacher, is to form and guide the immortal mind.

She, more than any one else, is to decide the character of her helpless children, both for this and the future eternal life. And for this, liberal provision should be made; so that no woman shall finish her education till all that science and training can do shall be bestowed to fit her for this supernal duty. The preparation of young ministers for the duties of the church does not surpass in importance the training of the minister of the nursery and school-room. The clergyman meets his parishioners two or three times a week to train them for an immortal existence. But the mother and school-teacher have their ministry in charge every hour of the day, and with a power of influence such as no clergyman can command.

In this review of the varied and complicated duties of a woman's profession, we find that she needs not only the general discipline and training for the development of mental faculties, but a special training for a far greater diversity of duties than are ever to be undertaken by men. We claim that woman's profession demands such very diverse training from the professions of the other sex that access to universities for men does not meet her most sacred necessities. A university education for woman should be as diverse from that of man's as are her duties and responsibilities.

We will now notice what has been done to prepare young men for their several professions, that we may sustain our position, that such advantages are unjustly withheld from their sisters, and that this has engendered multiplied evils to our sex, and thus to the commonwealth.

The mode of providing for the professions of men has been, not to trust chiefly to tuition fees for the support of instructors, but to secure the highest class of teachers by endowments insuring a salary independent of popular whims and changes. By means of such endowment, such *a division of labor and responsibility* is secured that each teacher is responsible for only one or two branches of instruction, and to only *one* class, and for only one or two hours each day.

The president of a college teaches only one class, and has no care or responsibility as to the proper performance of the several professors. Each professor has charge of only one class in one or two branches, and is responsible for only those branches; while neither president nor any other officer has any control or responsibility except in his own department. For the president is only *primus inter pares* (first among equals) as presiding officer of a faculty, in which every question is decided by majority vote. He has not (as do principals of most female colleges) the selection and direction of all the teachers, the supervision of finance and expenditure, the authority to inspect and control in every department, and the regulation of all salaries and expenditures for apparatus and libraries.

By this college method, every professor is made the honorable and independent controller of his own department, responsible to no one but the corporation or trustees. By this method, each teacher having in charge only one or two classes, and a single department, is able to devote much time to self-improvement and the advancement of his specialty.

Endowments also render the college permanent in its course of instruction and in retaining a permanent faculty, which can never be the case in schools that must change with every changing principal.

Endowments also open avenues of honor and support to large numbers of young men who eventually become professors, or who are stimulated to exertion by the hope of winning such permanent and honorable positions. No such opening for independence is provided for women.

Endowments have secured to young men not only a thorough training in branches of literature and science which enlarge the mental powers, but also have served to honor and elevate several of the trades and professions to which they are devoted, so that they are now on an honorable equality with the so-called liberal professions. The scientific schools, the art schools, and the schools of technology are fast elevating many heretofore degraded professions to equal honor with law, medicine, and divinity. The more these various arts and professions are made honorable by endowments to support learned professors, the larger the number of honorable and remunerative professions are provided for young men; and, as yet, woman (with one or two exceptions) has had no such opportunities provided. To support such institutions for young men, every State in the Union has been taxed, and large grants of land made by the general government, while individual benefactions have been still more abundant. Our oldest colleges all count their endowments as valued from half a million to four and five millions each. There are now more than two hundred well endowed colleges and scientific schools for young men, supporting many hundred professors. The State of New-York has twelve endowed colleges, having doubled the number in twenty years. Connecticut has three endowed colleges, and four endowed professional schools. Massachusetts has four colleges and six professional schools for young men, and other States in similar proportions.

As a contrast to this liberal provision for young men, I may be allowed to narrate some of my own experience. When I commenced my profession as teacher, the most popular boarding-schools taught little except the primary branches, though occasionally was executed by the pupils a "mourning piece," that is, an embroidered tombstone under an apparition by courtesy called a weeping willow, with a row of darkly-clad weeping friends approaching it. I was among the first to introduce what are called the higher branches. My school soon numbered over one hundred; and yet I had only one room and one assistant, while I had both to teach the higher branches and to study them myself; not having been taught them in my school days. I also had to prepare my teachers, who like myself had never been trained for these departments. And as my school rose in popularity, other schools followed the example, so that as fast as I trained reliable teachers, they were drawn off by the offers of higher salaries.

Meantime all the responsibilities, which in colleges are divided among the president, the professors, the tutors, and the treasurer, rested on me. Ten years of such complicated labor, study, and responsibility destroyed health, as it has done for multitudes of other women, who have thus toiled unaided by any of the advantages given to college teachers.

Ever since that time, I have devoted my income, strength, and time to efforts for securing professional advantages of education for my sex equal to those bestowed on men. It is over forty years that these efforts have been continued. And now, after remarkable and unexpected restoration to health, the institution I founded so many years ago is again committed to my charge.

In all this period, not a single institution has been founded which includes in its curriculum the course of practical training that prepares a woman for the complicated responsibilities I have enumerated as included in her profession. The Mount Holyoke plan does not even aim at any thing of this kind, but is only a method of economy to lessen expenditure. Vassar College has no endowment to support teachers, and so its tuition fees far exceed those of colleges for men. Nor is the industrial training of woman for her distinctive profession any part of its aim, while the largest portion of the income of that institution goes for the support of men instead of women teachers, five out of seven professors being men. And the excuse for this is, that well-trained female teachers can not be found, and so more highly educated men must be taken. But if woman had received the advantages given to men, most of these honorable and remunerative positions would have been hers.

The fact that men have been so much more highly educated in literature and science than women, causes the unjust discrimination in giving men the most honorable and remunerative positions even in female schools, where women equal or surpass them as successful teachers; so also in the comparatively unjust wages given to them in public schools.

The history of some of the most prominent female institutions shows that women are equal if not superior to men, in ability to educate their own sex, even when so little has been done for them and so much for men. For example, about the time I commenced my school, Mrs. Willard petitioned the Legislature of New-York to bestow some endowments on her flourishing institution, but without success; and yet without any such aid that institution has carried out a high course of literary education for woman, has had uninterrupted success, and still offers equal advantages with most female colleges where college-trained men are the chief recipients of the income, and are chief managers.

The Ingham University, of Central New-York, was founded by two women, and when it numbered over two hundred, sought endowments in vain. A man was then placed at its head, hoping thus to gain endowments; but under his administration the institution ran down, and was restored to prosperity only by restoration to woman's care.

The institution I founded at Hartford has always run down with college-educated men as principals, and flourished most under the charge of women.

The Milwaukee Female College, established by my influence, rose to prosperity under women, failed under a man, and was restored to prosperity by a woman.

The Mount Holyoke Female Seminary was founded by a woman, and has been sustained forty years by women alone. In all these cases, the men had a college education, and the women gained an education chiefly by unaided personal efforts. I think similar illustrations can be found all over the nation.

It is the unvarying testimony of the supervisors of public schools that women teachers are equal to men in ability and success, and yet to men, as the general rule, are given the best places and the largest salaries. While so many avenues to wealth and honor are open to men and so few to women, all will allow, that this is neither just nor generous, and if women can do so well at such disadvantage, what would they do if equal in privileges?

To illustrate still further the unjust discrimination in educational advantages, I will state that in Hartford, close beside my institution, is a college founded at nearly the same time, the numbers being about the same as in my school. The president teaches only one or two hours a day, and has no responsibility for any department except his own. The college treasurer has all the care of the finances, and, having endowments for this purpose, pays salaries to the president and five or six other teachers which would provide a house and support for a family to each. There are only four classes, and each teacher is required to instruct only one or two hours a day, having the remaining time for self-improvement and for literary labor to add to his income.

In the same city is a theological seminary with only twenty-five young men.[1] For them are provided spacious accommodations, with furniture frequently provided by generous women. Women also are among the most liberal founders of those endowments, valued at nearly or quite half a million, by which four professors and their families are supported and the board and expenses of a good portion of the pupils are paid. In Middletown is another endowed theological seminary, where ten instructors are provided for only thirty-six students. At New-Haven is another endowed theological seminary, where six instructors are employed to teach fifty-two young men, and so endowed that four professors and their families are supported by funds. And in all these cases, each professor teaches only one or two hours a day in only one or two branches. And in more than half the States of our Union, are similar institutions to train young men for church ministries, a large portion of them largely endowed by women; while not even one has yet been established to train woman for her no less sacred ministry.

When I took charge of the Hartford Female Seminary, this fall, the trustees and former principal had established a course of study, and pupils were preparing to graduate as in past time; while many reasons were urged for making no great changes.

---

[1] These statistics are taken from the Report of the National Bureau of Education for 1870.

The list of branches to be taught, as exhibited in the circular, is no larger than is common in many women high-schools and colleges, each one requiring a text-book, and reads thus: Spelling, reading, writing, grammar, arithmetic, higher arithmetic, algebra, history of the United States, physiology, physical geography, geometry, natural philosophy, chemistry, astronomy, mental philosophy, Butler's Analogy of Natural and Revealed Religion, æsthetics, English literature, history of Greece, history of Rome, philology, ancient and modern history, composition, natural history, history of England, history of France, botany, geology, rhetoric, trigonometry, moral philosophy, history of literature, history of arts and sciences, Latin, Greek, French, German, Italian, Spanish, drawing, painting in water-colors, painting in oil, vocal music, instrumental music, and gymnastics; *forty-four* in the whole.

For all these I am responsible to select teachers, to examine text-books, to decide on the modes of teaching, and to see that all departments are administered properly.

I can not carry out all these without at least seven English teachers, and four or five for the languages and accomplishments. And in arranging classes in so many branches, these teachers, on an average, must teach four or five hours a day, and have charge of six or seven classes in nearly as many different studies.

Though tuition charges have ever been larger than young men pay in colleges, in my former experience forty years ago, I could not retain the best teachers and furnish apparatus and advantages needed, only by using the whole income, except what I paid for my own board and my very economical personal expenses. And now, the income from one hundred pupils would not save me from embarrassing debt had I not other resources.

If I worked my teachers at the risk of their health, and employed those of humbler qualifications, I might, perhaps, make a small profit, but not otherwise. And as fast as teachers are trained, so as to be most valuable, (as in my earlier experience,) they will leave for posts offering higher pay and less labor. Neither Mrs. Stowe, nor myself, nor any of the most highly qualified ladies of our country, could take charge of such an institution without a sacrifice of an income counting by thousands. Will not a time come when ladies, the most highly qualified to educate their own sex, shall receive such advantages and compensation for these duties as now are exclusively given to men? My extensive acquaintance with ladies of this class all over the land enables me to predict an abundant supply of highly-trained educators to the duties of our sex, if the appropriate facilities, such as college professors obtain, were offered to them. But to take such a post as I now occupy, or to become a hard-working, ill-paid subordinate, or to become a family assistant, would not tempt them from present advantages of usefulness, independence, and comfort.

The present agitation as to woman's rights and wrongs is the natural and necessary result of the want of appreciation and neglect of the claims and duties of the family state. It is the manifest design of our Creator that each man should seek a wife and establish a family. And the family state has two ends to be accomplished; one is the increase and perpetuity of our race, and the other is its education and training; not chiefly to enjoy this life, but mainly to form a character that will secure endless happiness in the life to come.

The distinctive feature of the family state is, *the training of a small number by self-sacrificing labor and love*. Abraham, the friend of God, and the great model of faith and obedience to both Jews and Christians, was not allowed to have a child of his own till he had trained six hundred servants, each man dwelling in his tent with a family of his own, forming a religious community that obeyed the true God. This shows that it was not for personal gratification as the chief end that God instituted the family, and that those who are childless may have as great a work to perform as the parental.

But the more our nation has advanced in wealth and civilization, the more have the labors and the duties of the family state been shunned. Many virtuous young men are withheld from it from the incompetence and the extravagant habits and tastes of those they would otherwise seek for wives. Another class is withheld by guilty courses that destroy the hope of family love and purity. Another large class shun the toil, self-denial, and trials of married life, and prefer their ease and the many other enjoyments wealth will secure.

To these add the hundreds of thousands of young men who perished in our destructive war, and the emigration to new settlements where early marriage is impracticable, and as the consequence, the census shows hundreds of thousands of women who can never commence the family state as wife and mother. This is the great emergency that agitates society and forms the chief moral problem of our age. The question in its simplest form is this, What is to be done to secure the highest usefulness and happiness of *woman as a sex*, when marriage and the family state are more and more passing away? Our customs and our laws are all framed on the assumption that women are to be supported by husbands to rear up families; and yet marriage and the family state are more and more avoided. And what is the remedy to be sought? Will the ballot relieve this difficulty? Can any laws be enforced that will oblige men to marry? and if not, what are we to do to meet the emergency?

In reply, I will first state some important facts developed here in Massachusetts, where well-educated marriageable women most abound; not in employments for which God designed them, but in shops and mills and employment detrimental both to health and morals.

The report of the Massachusetts Board of State Charities states that the present mode of collecting special classes of the helpless, the unfortunate, and the vicious into great establishments, managed by paid agents, is not the best method to secure their physical, moral, and social improvement, and that it involves many unfortunate influences.

Then it is suggested that the better way would be to scatter these helpless and unfortunate ones in families of Christian people. Now, as before stated, the family is God's mode of training our race to self-denying love and labor; and the *Christian* family, in contrast to the worldly, is the one in which a small number is given to one or two, who have the spirit of Christ and live as he lived, to labor for others, and not for self-indulgent ease and worldly enjoyments.

Hundreds of Massachusetts women have this spirit of Christ and are pining for this ministry, which is as sacred and as effective as that of the church. Thousands of neglected orphans, or worse than orphans, abound on every side. The homeless, the aged, the weak, the sick, and the sinful, also, are all around us.

And how can truly Christian homes be established where there are no young children to train, no aged persons to watch over, no invalids to nurse, and no vicious to reclaim? Why are orphans thrown upon the cold world, and why are the aged held in a useless, suffering life except to furnish opportunities for Christian love and self-sacrifice? Here is the problem for Massachusetts. Let her do for her daughters as liberally as for her sons, and it will speedily be solved.

There are multitudes of women in unwomanly employments, who, if educated to the scientific duties of a nurse for young infants and their mothers, with all the advantages of high culture given to medical men, and with the social honor accorded to high culture, would be greeted in many a family, be sought as the most welcome benefactors of the family state, and take a superior position to that now given to the teachers of music, French, and drawing.

Again, there is no agent of the family state who has a more constant, daily influence on the character of childhood than the one who shares with a mother the cares of the nursery. And yet where shall we find an institution in which young women are properly trained for these sacred offices? The heir of an earthly kingdom is surrounded by the noblest and the wisest, who deem the humblest office an honor in his service. But the young heir of an immortal kingdom, whose career, not for a few earthly days, but for eternal ages, is to be decided in this life, to whom is he committed, and *where* and *how* were they trained for these supernal duties? The bogs of Ireland—the shanty tenement-houses—the plantation huts—the swarming, poverty-stricken wanderers from Europe, China, and Japan are coming to reply!

The influx of wealth, the building of expensive houses demanding many servants, and the increasing demands of social life, are changing mothers from the educational training of their own offspring to the training and care of servants; and yet, in our boarding-schools and colleges for women, how much is done to train them for such duties?

When I read the curriculum of Vassar and other female colleges, methinks their graduates by such a course as this will be as well prepared to nurse the sick, train servants, take charge of infants, and manage all departments of the family state, as they would be to make and regulate chronometers, or to build and drive steam-engines.

The number of branches introduced into female schools has nearly doubled since I commenced my school, while the real advantages gained by this increase have been lessened. And as yet little or no progress has been made in preparing women for the practical duties of their profession. The expenses of most popular boarding-schools confine their advantages to the rich, who do not aim to have daughters trained to do woman's work, or to earn their own independence.

The evils that women suffer from the want of proper training for their appropriate duties, few can fully realize. The Working-Woman's Union, in New-York City, reports that of the 13,000 applicants for work, not one half were qualified to any kind of work in a proper manner. The societies for aiding poor women report as their greatest embarrassment that but few can sew decently, or do any other work properly. The heads of dress-making establishments complain that few can be found who can be trusted to complete a dress properly, and say that those properly trained find abundant work and good pay. The demand for good mantua-makers in country towns is universal. In former days, plain sewing was taught in schools; but now it is banished, and mothers are too pressed with labor, or too negligent, to supply the deficiency.

In the middle classes, unmarried women and widows feel that they are an incumbrance on fathers and brothers, who, from pride or duty, feel bound to support them, and yet no openings offer for them to earn an independence. Thousands of ladies of good families and good education, with aged mothers or young children to support, can find either no employments or those offering starvation wages. The school or the boarding-house is the chief alternative for such persons; and yet every opening for a school-teacher has scores, and sometimes hundreds of applicants.

The factory-girls, and those in shops and stores, must stand six, eight, or ten hours a day in bad air and unwholesome labor. The influx of ignorant and uncleanly foreigners into our kitchens, and the exactions of thriftless young housekeepers from boarding-schools, drive self-respecting American women from many of our kitchens.

Meantime, in our more wealthy classes, those who have generous and elevated aspirations feel that they have no object in life—no profession, like their brothers, by which they can secure their own independence, and aid in elevating others. Our young girls are trained only for marriage; and when that fails, fathers and brothers forbid their earning an independence, as implying disgrace to themselves.

The remedy for all this would soon be achieved were woman's work elevated to an honorable and remunerative science and profession, by the same methods that men have taken to elevate their various professions. The establishment of *Woman's Universities*, in which every girl shall secure as good a literary training as her brothers, and then be trained to some profession adapted to her taste and capacity, by which she can establish a home of her own, and secure an independent income—*this* is what every woman may justly claim and labor for, as the shortest, surest, and safest mode of securing her own highest usefulness and happiness, and that of her sex; a mode which demands only what, if once achieved as practicable, every intelligent and benevolent man would approve and delight to promote.

Here I feel bound to express dissent from the frequent implication that men are alone responsible for the present disabilities and wrongs of woman, owing to a selfish and tyrannical spirit not existing in my sex. There is no nation in the world, and never has been one, in which all classes of men were so trained to honor, protect, and provide for women as in our own. On the contrary, women with us have been trained to expect care and protection, and not to a chivalrous and tender regard for their own sex, such as has been cultivated in brothers, fathers, and husbands.

Moreover, women are trained to economy in details more than men, and have not the free use of money as have those who earn family support. As a consequence, when the raising of the wages of a school-teacher, or the charges of a seamstress, or the pay of a cook is discussed, it is often the case that women are no more ready than men thus to increase the advantages of their sex.

In the matter of educational benefactions, women have given liberally to endow colleges and professional schools for men; and it is a remarkable fact that, if we except Roman Catholic nunneries, I know not of even one case in this nation where a woman is supported as an educator by an endowment given by a woman.

As previously indicated, the main causes of the evils that now press on my sex are the want of appreciation of the honor and duties of the family state, and the decrease of marriage, owing to war, emigration, self-indulgence, and vices consequent on increase of civilization and wealth.

There is every evidence that men are as sympathetic, and as anxious to devise remedies for the evils complained of, as are our own sex; and the impolitic and unjust manner in which they have been treated by some who are generously laboring for the relief and elevation of woman, is greatly to be regretted. In all my past efforts, I have depended mainly on the powerful influence of my sex in gaining what was sought; for I believe there is no benevolent plan, which is so approved by judicious and benevolent women as to secure their earnest efforts, which will not receive from fathers, brothers, and husbands all that is sought. My only difficulty in the past has been to secure such appreciation from my sex of the honor and duties of the family state, of the need of scientific and practical training for these duties, as would secure their earnest attention, influence, and efforts.

While I would urge these views on the attention of all women who have any influence, I beg leave to suggest other modes by which the same ends may be promoted. Thus, every cultivated woman who dignifies domestic labor, by living in such a style as enables her to work herself, and to train her sons and daughters to work with her, is a co-laborer in this beneficent enterprise. Every woman who goes to her kitchen in the spirit of Christ, by self-denying efforts to train her servants to intelligence, honesty, and benevolence, is another blessed laborer on the same field. Every young lady who seeks to impart some of her advantages to those who labor in her service will be preparing to hear from their and her Lord, "Inasmuch as ye did it to these the least of my brethren, ye did it to me." Every school-teacher who trains her pupils to value home labor, and to learn to do all woman's proper work in the best manner, is also a minister of good to the family state. Every woman who uses her influence to introduce sewing into public schools, or to establish sewing-schools among the poor, is another co-laborer for the same high aim. Every woman who can bring the views here presented to the notice of wealthy and influential men and women, may be sowing seed that will yield rich fruits even for ages to come, by endowments secured through such quiet influences.

A Woman's University, that will realize the ideal aimed at, may, perhaps, come by no sudden growth, but by many experiments in different fields and diverse departments, each aiding to advance every other, till all eventually will be combined in a harmonious and perfected result. And for this consummation my good friend and opponent is as ready to labor as those of us who have not her courage and hopes as to the results of woman suffrage.

I stated that I have resumed the charge of the seminary I founded forty years ago, to teach the higher branches, with Mrs. Stowe, then, as now, my associate. We began when women were trained to domestic labor, and almost nothing else. We have seen the pendulum swing to the other extreme, till, both in families and schools, women are taught the higher branches, and almost nothing else. We now begin at the other end, and, by the aid and counsel of the judicious women of Hartford, we hope to set an example of a woman's university which shall combine the highest intellectual culture with the highest practical skill in all the distinctive duties of womanhood.

Our good friends of the women suffrage cause often liken their agitation to that which ended the slavery of a whole race doomed to unrequited toil for selfish, cruel masters. When so many men are toiling to keep daughters, wives, and mothers from any kind of toil, it is difficult to trace the resemblance.

Moreover, we of the other side are believers in slavery, and we mean to establish it all over the land. We mean to force men to resign their gold, and even to forge chains for themselves with it; and when we have trained their fair and rosy daughters, we will enforce a "Pink and White Tyranny" more stringent than any other earthly thraldom. And we will make our slaves work, and work from early dawn to dark night, under the Great Task-master, the Lord of love and happiness, until every one on earth shall fear him, as "the beginning of wisdom;" and then "do justly, love mercy, and walk humbly with God," as the whole end and perfection of man.

For want of time, only a part of this address was delivered at the Boston Music Hall. Mrs. Livermore followed, and at Note A are remarks in reply to some of hers. What follows will present further views on the subject of Woman's Profession.

After resigning the charge of the Hartford Female Seminary, many circumstances combined to give me unusual facilities for observing educational influences in various institutions for both sexes.

Continued ill health led to extensive travels, and to protracted visits to a widely dispersed family and to former pupils settled in every section of the country. My father was president of a theological seminary, and my brother-in-law has been professor in two colleges and one theological seminary. One brother was valedictorian and tutor at Yale, and then president of one of the first Western colleges. Six brothers were educated in five different colleges, and thirteen nephews were students in six different colleges. Thirty-four nieces and nephews have been connected with a great number of different boarding-schools as scholars or teachers, while several hundred of my former pupils have been teachers or pupils in almost every State of the Union, and have extensively reported to me their experiences and observations.

I have also been connected with two organizations for establishing schools and female colleges in such a way as to make it a part of my duties to select teachers for schools and to organize faculties for large female institutions.

These opportunities, extended over a period of nearly forty years, have secured principles and conclusions of such importance as warrants not only general statements, but some details to illustrate.

A fundamental principle thus gained is, that the school should be an appendage of the family state, and modeled on its primary principle, which is, *to train the ignorant and weak by self-sacrificing labor and love; and to bestow the most on the weakest, the most undeveloped, and the most sinful.*

It is exactly the opposite course to which teachers are most tempted. The bright, the good, the industrious are those whom it is most agreeable to teach, who win most affection, and who most promote the reputation of a teacher and of a school or college. To follow this principle, therefore, demands more clear views of duty and more self-denying benevolence than ordinarily abound.

Moreover, the common practice of schools and colleges is, after a certain amount of trial, to turn out those who are too dull to reach a given line of scholarship, or too mischievous to conform to rules. It is assumed that the interests of the more intelligent and docile are to override those of the stupid and disobedient, and that schools and colleges are not to adopt the great principle illustrated in the story of the prodigal son, the strayed lamb, and the heavenly joy over one that was lost more than over the ninety and nine that went not astray.

The results of attempts to carry out this divine principle in school management, in my earlier years, were very encouraging. The frequent teachers' meetings were made the means of discovering the intellectual and moral deficiencies of each pupil, and then the difficult cases were apportioned to the care and watch of the several teachers, according to their adaptation to the duty assigned. Each was to consult and devise methods, report to me, and to receive counsel from me as to further measures. A few specific cases will illustrate some results.

For example, one of our best pupils and very intelligent in certain directions, was reported as utterly incapable of understanding the reasoning process in geometry. After experiments for more than a year, this pupil became not only one of our best mathematical scholars, but one of our most successful teachers in that study.

In another case, the pupil was one of a numerous class that have imagination and fancy undeveloped and apparently wanting, having little or no appreciation of poetry, fine writing, or works of imagination. A long course of discipline and practice so developed these dormant powers that this pupil not only became an admirer and critic of poetry and fine writing, but presented, as her closing public exercise, a specimen of poetry, devised and completed without aid, which would favorably compare with half of that which is written and admired in our current literature.

In other cases, in my school and among my friends, I have noticed that, while some children have all the mental faculties equally developed, others appear to possess small capacities, except in one or two directions, which in some cases are prominent and in others so undeveloped as to appear wanting.

For example, the son of a dear friend had been trained by good teachers and sent to a first-class college, where every ordinary method was employed to carry him through with at least moderate respectability, and all proved an utter failure. The young man was then placed with a good private teacher, who, after repeated experiments, ascertained that in certain directions the mental faculties were above mediocrity, but in points not reached by college training. Another method was adopted, and the result was, that the young man became distinguished in one branch of practical science, and eventually a popular and successful professor in a scientific school.

In treating both intellectual and moral deficiencies, great attention and care are demanded, so as not to deal with the willing but weak as with the careless or mischievous. Both efforts demand the labor of self-sacrificing love, and the rewards for such efforts have been witnessed in such abundance as to cause great regret that so seldom our higher schools and colleges aim at such results.

Another very important principle, especially in the training of women, is, that the duties of the family state, as performed when parents and children are united in domestic labors, have a direct and very decided influence in training the intellectual powers.

In such families, the first-born, especially if a daughter, begins almost in infant days to aid the mother in the care of the younger. Discretion, quickness, invention, and many other faculties are cultivated in the care of the little one, in regulating its caprices and controlling its mischievous impulses. She learns to wash and dress a younger child, to execute contrivances for its amusement, to regulate its habits, and to aid as a teacher in its first school lessons. She is trained to sew, mend, and to make family clothing, and then to aid in teaching these arts to the younger. The first rudiments of culture in the fine arts commence when assisting in ornamenting garden and parlor with flowers and with various contrivances. She learns to cook food, and to understand the varieties and the modes of preservation. And so of many other household duties which demand quickness of apprehension, discretion, energy, and perseverance. It is an unconscious intellectual training, usually enforced by limited means, and insuring benefits which the offspring of the rich rarely enjoy.

It is on this principle that Frobel arranged his system of the Kindergarten, which develops many mental faculties and trains to intellectual exercises before book knowledge is sought, chiefly by exercises that cultivate taste, ingenuity, contrivance, and skill in the use of the hand and eye.

The early training in my own personal and family history is a remarkable illustration of this principle. This was at a time when book-learning for the young was at its lowest stage. The whole of my childhood was a play-spell, where my chief contrivances were to avoid all kinds of confinement to study, or any kind of intellectual taxation, except in practical employments, for which happily I had a decided taste.

The death of a wise and tender mother at sixteen, and the consequent responsibilities that came on the eldest of eight children, still further developed the intellectual powers which are cultivated in domestic employments. But school duties were never relished, except as opportunities of furnishing merriment and various amusing contrivances for escaping study. No discipline by book knowledge was gained, and no reading attempted except in works of imagination.

It was not till school-days were over, that the discipline of sorrow, and the consequent forces of religion, sobered an exuberant nature and led to preparation for the office of a teacher.

Then, for the first time, commenced a training in book knowledge under the care of a college-trained brother, and then a few months accomplished what, with most school-girls, demands as many years. And this speed and success were secured by aid of faculties developed and strengthened chiefly by domestic training, together with the conversation and intellectual influence of the parents and family friends who were my educators.

The mental history of these family friends is an additional illustration of this principle. My father had a college education; my mother and an aunt, who was a member of our family, had only that of a country home, when reading, writing, and arithmetic were the only branches in children's schools. My mother had a natural taste for profound investigation, and, with no aid but a small encyclopedia, performed some remarkable mathematical calculations where my father was helpless. But apparently she had no talent for poetry or fine writing, though having a high appreciation of both. On the contrary, my aunt was a fine writer, and composed poetry of a high order. Both the ladies were extensive readers of the best English classics, much more so than my father.

And now in my recollections of home discussions, and of the admiration universally accorded to my mother's intellectual gifts, I should say that by the common school, by domestic duties, by English literature, and by the sciences studied in one small encyclopedia and two or three other scientific books, my mother was, if not superior, fully equal to my father in mental power and culture. And in fine writing and most æsthetic developments my aunt was superior to both, though she was their inferior in several other directions.

Moreover, five of my father's sons were trained in the best colleges, while his daughters all knew little or nothing of the chief branches included in the college course. And yet the domestic training of the daughters and their more extensive reading, as I view it, made them fully equal to my brothers in intellectual development.

Similar observations met me in general society when comparing the mental development of sisters having only a common school education with that of college-trained brothers, and this at all periods and in every direction. And it is in view of such multiplied illustrations that I understand how it is that women, with much fewer advantages of classic and mathematical training than college graduates enjoy, prove better educators than men for children and for the more mature of their own sex.

Here I wish it to be understood, that my aim in remarks on colleges is not to present their advantages or deficiencies, except so far as they are influencing female institutions to the same courses of study and organization. I am not qualified to advise as to institutions for men; but the profession and pursuits of women as a sex are to be so widely diverse from those of men that they should secure as diverse methods of training.

I regard the effort to introduce women into colleges for young men as very undesirable, and for many reasons. That the two sexes should be united, both as teachers and pupils, in the same institution seems very desirable, but rarely in early life by a method that removes them from parental watch and care, and the protecting influences of a home.

There will always be exceptional cases when children have no suitable parents or guardians; while at a maturer period, after the principles and habits are largely solidified, there are advantages in sending a child from home. The true method, at the immature periods of life, is the union of the home and the school in protecting from dangers and in forming good habits and principles.

I have repeatedly resided in the immediate vicinity of boarding-schools for boys, embracing the children of my relatives or intimate friends, and never without wonder and distress at the risks to some and the ruin to others constantly going on. Such institutions always have had inmates shrewd and often malignant, while the rash curiosity of youth is ready to meet any danger.

Withdrawn from parents and sisters, and all home influences, the young boy is lodged, often in isolated dormitories or in negligent private families, with classmates of all kinds of habits. And so tobacco, creating an unnatural thirst for other exciting stimulants, is secretly introduced; then alcoholic drinks; then the most gross and licentious literature; and all so secretly that teachers can not meet the evil. I have known these results repeatedly in schools under the most careful, pious, and celebrated teachers.

Thus, at the age most susceptible and most dangerous, the young boy is taken from mother and sisters and the safe guardianship of a home, and amid such perils committed to strangers who, with multitudinous pupils and cares, can give no special care to any one child.

Another general principle attained by my experience is, that both quickness of perception and retention of memory depend very greatly on the *degree of interest* excited. It is not the most learned teacher that always has most success in imparting permanent knowledge. As an illustration, when I commenced teaching Latin, it was under the care of a very accurate and faithful brother, who stood first in scholarship in Yale as valedictorian. I was then only a few pages ahead of my scholars in the *Liber Primus*, and yet, when they had finished most of Virgil and selections from Cicero, this brother and several other examiners said that they had never seen any classes of boys superior to my class in accurate and complete scholarship.

Even in the pronunciation of the French, I have found that it was not the best educated teacher, speaking with the purest Parisian accent, who was most successful, but rather a lady whose enthusiasm and perseverance and carefulness would not allow a single syllable to be mispronounced by her pupils. This explains how it is that women with less education so often prove more successful than men in managing female institutions.

By this same general principle of quickening intellect by exciting interest, I learned the importance of educating every young girl with some practical aim, by which, in case of poverty, she might support herself; and also, of selecting for this end some pursuit suited to her natural tastes and character. To study what is liked and with the hope of thus securing some agreeable and substantial advantage in future life more than doubles the interest, and thus quickens and exalts the intellectual powers.

In this view of the case, it became an important inquiry as to which of the employments and studies of our higher female seminaries could be made available in securing a remunerative profession to a woman, and one that would be suitable for her sex. Here, again, I may be allowed to introduce some of my own experience as guiding to a conclusion, at least in one particular.

All through my childhood, my father daily read the Bible, in course, at family prayers, and when his inquisitive children asked questions as to matters of delicacy, they were told that the Bible was given by God to instruct men in all their duties, and that some things were not for children to know till they were men and women; that this inquiry was about things they could not understand, and that it was wrong to try to do so.

After such wise training, my first experience as a teacher of Latin was to a class of young girls as ignorant as myself of all the wickedness of the world; and then I was plied with questions I could not answer except by aid of a brother; when to my dismay and disgust I found the worst vices of heathenism, and those most likely to tempt young boys, made respectable and attractive by the charms of classic poetry, and forming a part of a boy's training for college.

And here I would ask why it has come to pass that the Bible, in its original Greek, is turned out of the college course of most of our leading colleges, (for it formerly was required,) while the vulgarity and vice of heathenism are preserved and made attractive in fitting boys for college? Is it not time for woman to have a more decided ministry in training young boys for their college life? Should not women be trained in Latin and Greek, so that mothers and sisters thus taught could fit young boys for college, instead of sending them at the most perilous age away from the watch and care of a home and all female influence, to boys' boarding-schools, to mix with all sorts, and there be taught all manner of evil? Teachers trained in these languages could go into families to aid a mother in these duties, and would be liberally compensated. This, then, is a profession for which a woman can be trained even in our common schools as well as in female colleges.

Another very interesting fact revealed by personal experience is, that there is no knowledge so thorough and permanent as that gained in teaching others. Repeatedly, in my own case, and still oftener in the case of my teachers, has it been observed that a lesson or problem supposed to be comprehended, was imperfect, and corrected only in attempts to aid others in understanding it. In no other profession is the sacred promise, "Give and it shall be given unto you," so fully realized as in that of a teacher.

This view of the case has led me to devise methods by which every pupil, in school-days, shall have an opportunity to attempt to teach, and be taught how to do it in the best manner; and that, too, in every stage of advancement from lowest to highest. There are methods which secure this advantage with great economy of time and labor which can not be detailed here.

Another very important principle in acquiring knowledge is the taking of a few branches at one time, and especially in having these associated in their character, so that each is an assistance in understanding and remembering the other. For illustration, let geography, history, polite literature, and composition, for a certain period, be the leading studies of a class which has completed a short course in these studies in the preparatory school. Then let history be studied by successive periods, marked by some great events or by some distinguished characters; and as each country is introduced, let its civil, political, and physical geography be fully studied; its animals and productions be illustrated by drawings and by selection from travels read to the class; this might be done either in connection with the history or as a separate class in geography, conducted in connection with the class of history and reciting at a different hour.

At the same time, the teacher of the class in literature and *belles-lettres* could be presenting at another hour the state of science, literature, and the fine arts, with illustrative drawings, and also an account of the prominent learned men and authors of that period, with some account of their most celebrated works, reading some selections. For example, suppose, the period that of Alexander the Great, by this method, one teacher would introduce most of the geography of countries of the ancient world, while the literature and the fine arts of Greece in its palmy days would, under another teacher, be connected with the study of its history. At the same time the exercises in a daily class in composition might have topics and exercises to correspond.

So in the period of the crusades; in one class, the history would be studied; in another, the civil, political, and physical geography of the countries introduced; in another, the history of literature, the fine arts, and the distinguished authors, with some account of their works. This period might be still more vividly presented in standard works of fiction, such as Scott's *Talisman* and *Ivanhoe,* to be read in hours of social gathering or at home.

To make room for such a method, much of the minute and uninteresting details now so excessive in our geographies and histories, which are forgotten as soon as learned, would be omitted for these more valuable and more interesting exercises. On such a plan, the pupil would have three or four recitations on diverse topics, and yet so connected that each would illustrate and vivify the other, while the interest thus excited would make permanent in the memory all these details.

There is great loss of time and labor in the common method of pursuing four, five, or six disconnected branches of study. The mind is distracted by the variety, and feels a feeble and divided interest in all. In many cases, this method of *cramming* the mind with uninteresting and disconnected details serves to debilitate rather than to promote mental power. The memory is the faculty chiefly cultivated, and this at the expense of the others. This method has been greatly increased since the honors of graduating have become so popular in female colleges and high-schools.

The excess of uninteresting details is a serious objection to many text-books of history and geography. It is very much to be regretted that the plan introduced in Woodbridge and Willard's Geography, by which details are systematized under general heads, is so widely neglected.

No experience has been more valuable to me than that relating to physical training. Few are aware how much can be done in schools to promote development, health, and the proper and graceful use of the body and limbs. My residence in such a large number and variety of health establishments, in studying the causes and cure of the prevailing debility and diseases of American women, has led to the conviction that there are very few diseases or deformities which a teacher properly trained may not remedy by natural methods, and those which may be made a part of school training.

Here I would invite the special attention of mothers and teachers to a work on the Diseases of Women, by Dr. George H. Taylor, published by G. Maclean, 85 Nassau St., N. Y., in which such natural methods are presented, many of which can be employed in the family and school without the attendance of a physician.

In the early part of my school experience, a European lady artist of fine personal appearance offered to teach in my school a system of exercises by which she herself, once a humpback cripple, was restored to a perfect and graceful figure. These were disconnected exercises, one portion of which I introduced into my work on physiology and calisthenics as what could be easily used in all schools without demanding a separate room and dress for the purpose.

Other portions I combined into a system of calisthenic exercises *set to music,* and demanding a separate room, and this method was extensively introduced into schools until Dr. Dio Lewis prepared his system, now extensively used.

The difficulties of Dr. Lewis's method are, that it demands a separate dress and room for the purpose, which multitudes of schools will not adopt, and also is so violent as to endanger the health of delicate young girls, while it has but little tendency to promote ease and gracefulness of person and movements. For these reasons it is constantly passing out of use after a short trial.

In place of this, I have originated another method by which personal defects and deformities are remedied, and gracefulness in the movement of head, body, and limbs promoted. It includes exercises which *gently* train all the muscles, which are varied and entertaining, and which are performed to music, the pupils singing songs prepared for each exercise.

The results in curing defects and promoting health, ease, and gracefulness of movement and manner have been so remarkable as to excite some wonder that, even in dancing-schools, so little has been attempted in these particulars, when so much might be so easily effected. The proper and graceful mode of walking, sitting, and using the hands and arms is rarely taught in any schools. So, also, the training of the voice to agreeable tones and enunciation in conversation is almost never attempted, and yet few things have a more constant influence in giving pleasure.

The regulation and use of amusements as a part of education is, as yet, scarcely recognized as a school duty. There is nothing that gains more personal regard and influence with pupils than joining in their amusements, while opportunities are thus given to promote both health and literary improvement. And teachers need this kind of exercise and relaxation as much or more than their scholars.

One very valuable method is combining the reading of interesting works of fiction with the period of history pursued in school hours, and also with ornamental needle-work pursued while listening to reading. In long winter evenings, an hour for study, an hour for active amusements, and an hour for this kind of reading and needle-work would unite health, pleasure, and literary improvement in an unusual degree.

In resuming the religious training of an institution embracing pupils whose parents hold views differing essentially from mine, it becomes my duty to state the method I shall pursue. I propose to avoid all conflict with opinions taught to my pupils by their parents and clergymen. I shall simply take the teachings of Christ as my only guide, and present, as he did, "Our Father in heaven" as a kind and sympathizing parent, who loves and cares for *all* the children he has created more tenderly than any earthly parent can do; who ever is seeking their best good; who is pleased when they strive to do right, and grieved when they do wrong.

If any come to me for help in regard to theological doctrines, I shall teach them the simple laws of interpretation used in common life, and how to employ them in studying for themselves the teachings of the Bible. I shall assume the foundation principle of the teachings of Jesus Christ as the basis of religious training. I mean *the dangers of the future world*. For it was the prime object of his advent to teach us these dangers, and the way of escape.

Here I shall avoid all theories and all speculations, and confine myself strictly to *the facts* taught by Jesus Christ. I shall assume as true *the fact* revealed by the only person who has died and returned to this life to tell us what awaits us in that dark and silent land toward which we all are hastening; the solemn and dreadful *fact* that there are such awful dangers in the world to come that the chief end and aim of this life should be to save ourselves and all we can influence, and, if need be, at the sacrifice of every earthly plan and enjoyment.

Still more solemn to each individual mind is *the fact* taught by our Lord, that the number of those who escape an awful doom in the future life depends on the character and efforts of the followers of Christ.

I shall assume as true the *fact* revealed by Jesus Christ that the *only* way of salvation is by *faith* in our Creator; not a mere intellectual belief in his existence and laws, but a faith including this belief and also practical obedience to his laws; by *repentance*, not a mere emotion of sorrow, but including the ceasing of disobedience; by *love*, not chiefly emotional, but rather that which is thus defined by inspiration, "This is the love of God, that ye keep his commandments."

Obedience to the laws of our Creator, physical, social, and moral, being the chief element of the *faith, repentance,* and *love* by which alone we escape the dangers of the future world, the question will be urged as to *the degree* of obedience which will secure safety. Here we find in Christ's teachings that *perfect* obedience is not indispensable to salvation. The demand is that "the heart" (that is, the chief aim and interest) be devoted to such obedience. We are to "seek *first*" the kingdom of

God and *his righteousness*. And all who do this, in both the Old Testament and the New, are recognized as the righteous, as the children of God, and as heirs to the eternal blessedness of his kingdom.

It is the revelation of the dangers of the life to come which decides the character of the worldly educator in contrast to that of the Christian. The one has for the leading interest and aim to secure the enjoyments of this life; the other has as the chief interest and aim to follow Christ in self-denying labors to save as many as possible from the dangers of the life to come. The one lives as if there were little or no danger in the future world. The other toils, as if in the perils of a shipwreck, to save as many as possible and at whatever personal sacrifice of ease or worldly enjoyment. The one finds little occasion for self-sacrificing labors; the other is constantly aiming to save others from sin and its ruin by daily self-denying efforts.

It was "for the joy that was set before him" that "the Shepherd and Bishop of souls" "endured the cross, despising the shame." And when he invites his followers to take and bear the same cross, he encourages with the assurance that this yoke is easy and this burden light, and that it brings "rest to the soul."

And here, for the encouragement of my pupils and friends, I feel bound to give my testimony to the verity of these promises.

It is now more than forty years that my chief interest and aim has been to labor to save my fellow-men to the full extent of my power. To this end I have sacrificed all my time, all my income, my health, and every plan of worldly ease and pleasure. With sympathies that would naturally seek the ordinary lot of woman as the ideal of earthly happiness, with no natural taste for notoriety or public action, with tastes for art, and imaginative and quiet literary pursuits, I have, for all that period, been doing what, as to personal taste, I least wished to do, and leaving undone what I should most like to do. I have been for many years a wanderer without a home, in delicate health, and often baffled in favorite plans of usefulness. And yet my life has been a very happy one, with more enjoyments and fewer trials than most of my friends experience who are surrounded by the largest share of earthly gratifications. And since health is restored, except as I sympathize in the sorrows of others, I am habitually as happy as I wish to be in this world. And this is not, as some may say, the result of a happy temperament; for in early life, at its most favored period, I was happy chiefly by anticipations that were not realized, and never with that satisfying, peaceful enjoyment of the present, which is now secured, and is never to end.

The preceding views lead to inquiries of great practical importance, such as these:

Is it consistent with Christian principles to take children from the care of parents at the most critical period of life, and congregate them in large boarding-schools and colleges, where temptations multiply and individual love and care are diminished?

Is it practicable, in public and private schools, to institute methods by which each pupil shall be trained according to peculiar wants, so that deficient faculties shall be developed, and unfortunate intellectual, physical, and moral traits or habits be rectified?

Can such schools institute methods by which every pupil shall, at least, *commence* a training for some business in future life, to which natural abilities and tastes incline, and in which success would be most probable?

Can woman's distinctive profession be made a large portion of her school education?

To aid in deciding these questions, the following is given as the *ideal* at which I have been aiming in efforts to establish a *Woman's University*; by which I mean, not a large boarding-establishment of pupils removed from parental care, but an institution embracing the whole course of a woman's training from infancy to a self-supporting profession, in which both parents and teachers have a united influence and agency.

According to this ideal, such an institution would be divided into distinct schools; all under the same board of supervision, and all carrying out a connected and appropriate portion of the same plan. These are:

1. The *Kindergarten*, for the youngest children, who are not to use books;

2. The *Primary School*, for children just commencing the use of books;

3. The *Preparatory School*, introductory to the higher;

4. The *Collegiate School*, embracing a course of four years;

5. The *Professional School*, to prepare a woman for all domestic duties and for a self-supporting profession.

For the control of all these there would be such a *division of responsibilities* as follows:

1. The first would be the *department of intellectual training*; committed to a woman of high culture in every branch taught in the collegiate school; possessing quick discernment, intellectual and moral force, and great interest in her special department. To her would be committed the superintendence of all the schools, except the professional, and it would be her duty to secure *perfect lessons* from every pupil by the following method.

She would first gain from the teachers such an arrangement of lessons for every child as is fitted to its ability, and, if need be, have classes so divided that those of nearly equal ability shall be in one class, that the brighter or more advanced might not be retarded. Then, at the close of the daily school, it would be the duty of every teacher to send every pupil who has not a *perfect* lesson, whatever might be the cause, to the charge of this lady superintendent, who would keep them with her until each had studied and recited the imperfect lesson in the most satisfactory manner. By this method perfect lessons will be secured every day from every pupil.

It would also be her duty to carry out a method, which will not here be detailed, by which, after due training, every pupil shall occasionally act as teacher under her supervision. By this and another method, not here indicated, great economy of time will be secured to pupils who ordinarily are obliged to spend much time in recitation-rooms in hearing others recite, without any special benefit to themselves, and involving great trial of their patience, and also temptation to irregularities. Likewise it would be the duty of this teacher to ascertain intellectual defects, and adapt measures for the remedy; also to ascertain, by aid of both parents and teachers, natural tastes and aptitudes, with reference to special school-training in branches preparatory to a self-supporting profession.

2. The department of *moral training* would be given to a woman of high moral and mental culture, whose tastes, talents, and experience prepare her to excel in this department. It would be her duty to study the character and discover the excellences of every pupil, by aid both of the other teachers and the parents, and then to devise methods of improvement; instructing the other teachers how to aid in these efforts. She also would seek the aid and coöperation of the most mature and influential pupils, and direct them how to exert a coöperating influence. The general religious instruction of the institution also would be conducted under her supervision and control.

3. The department of the *physical training* of all the institution would be committed to a woman of good practical common sense, of refined culture and manners, and one expressly educated for this department. By the aid of both parents and teachers, she would study the constitution and habits of every pupil, and administer a method of training to develop healthfully every organ and function, and to remedy every defect in habits, person, voice, movements, and manners.

Here I would remark that my extensive investigations in many health-establishments as to the causes of the decay of female health, and my extensive opportunities for gaining the opinions and counsels of the most learned and successful physicians of all schools, lead me to the belief that there are few chronic maladies, deformities, or unhealthful habits that may not be entirely remedied by a system of physical exercise and training *in schools*, under the charge of a woman properly qualified for these duties.

If a similar officer were provided for our colleges, whose official duty should be to train the body to health, strength, grace, and good manners, should we not see much fewer sallow faces, round shoulders, projecting necks, shambling gaits, awkward gestures, and gawky and slovenly manners, such as now too frequently mark the college-graduate? Why have the heathen youth of ancient Greece so excelled those of our age and religion in manly strength, beauty, and grace?

And if a department in colleges should be instituted, on the plan here indicated for *moral training*, would not the barbarous and vulgar practices that so often degrade the manners, and endanger life and limb, be ended?

It is a great evil in many of our colleges and professional schools, that when a professor has once gained his chair, no degree of dullness or neglect will oust him, especially if supported by nepotism or a clique. This I have so often heard reported of institutions with which my family and personal friends have been connected, that it would seem as if few such institutions escaped this evil. And it seems to be one which might be remedied by means of such an officer as has been described as head of the department of intellectual training, whose official duty it should be to examine every department and report deficiencies to the faculty and corporation for remedy.

In this connection I would entreat special attention to the perils of young girls in most large boarding-schools, and such as are little realized. The collecting of many into buildings and rooms imperfectly warmed and ventilated, the overtasking the brain by excessive study, the excitements of boarding-school life in contrast to home quietude, the unhealthful food and condiments bought at shops or sent from home and distributed to companions, the want of proper healthful exercise, the want of maternal watch and care at critical periods and at commencing disease, the debilitating practices taught at the most dangerous period to the ignorant by the thoughtless or vicious, and many other unfortunate influences, combine to a greater or less extent in all large boarding-schools.

Having had charge of one myself for nearly ten years, in which, as it seemed to me, every thing was done that could be to abate such evils, I have concluded that such institutions for both boys and girls may be called successful only on the same calculation as would be made in cultivating a garden on the top of a house. The best of soil, seed, manure, and labor, with water and sun and awnings, may be provided, and yet the proper place to make a good garden is on mother earth. And so the proper place to educate children before maturity is under the mother's care, with the coöperating aid of a school.

If I could narrate one half of the sad histories of the ruined boys and girls, and the consequent agonies from blasted parental hopes, that have come to my personal knowledge, where health or morals, or both, were destroyed for a whole life at large boarding-schools, this false and fatal method would be greatly abated.

And here I would direct attention to one item so pernicious, and yet so common and so misunderstood as to excite constant wonder and regret as connected with boarding institutions for both sexes, and that is *the want of effective methods for providing pure air*. In private families, only a few lungs vitiate the inhaled air; but the larger the number in one building, the larger are the arrangements needed for emptying out the foul air and introducing the pure.

An open fire is a sure and certain method. But when buildings are warmed by hot-air furnaces, or by hot-water or steam-pipes, the almost inevitable results are pernicious. In the case of heated air from a furnace, it always will find exit from a building in the shortest or most available direction, and then all the rooms not in this line of draught will have the air nearly stationary, to be breathed over and over again by their inmates.

Heating by steam or by hot-water pipes involves still greater difficulties, when no arrangement is made for carrying off the foul air, inasmuch as it is the air *in* the house which is heated without introducing pure air.

This is the most dangerous of all methods of warming when there is no connected ventilating arrangement, while it is the best and most agreeable of all methods when properly managed. Mr. Lewis Leeds, ventilating engineer in New-York City, has invented the following method. The coils of steam or hot-water pipes are placed close to a window, with an opening at the bottom of it, regulated by a register which admits pure air directly on to the coils, and thus it is warmed.

Thus a person can sit by the coils and secure radiated heat as from a fire, have the light of the window and the influx of perfectly pure and yet warm air. In addition, every room has an opening both at top and bottom into a warm-air flue, through which the impure air of the room is constantly carried off.

Any room can be perfectly ventilated which has openings at the top and bottom of a flue, through which warm air is passing. But no flues filled with cold air will ventilate a room, though housebuilders, and householders, and school committees have been ignorantly providing such useless arrangements all over the land.

And here I affirm with heart-felt sorrow that never, in a single instance, have I known or even heard of a large boarding-school with any proper arrangements for ventilation. Even Vassar College, now so extensively regarded as a model institution, has adopted the most dangerous mode of warming without any arrangement but doors and windows to supply pure air to its recitation-rooms and sleeping-rooms.

And so, as in all similar cases, the strong and well, who are distressed for want of pure air, will have windows open, and then the delicate, who are not inured to sudden changes or to great extremes, will take colds. There is no doubt that the reports of the miasmatic diseases and lung affections of teachers and pupils in this institution have been greatly exaggerated; but not because there has not been abundant reason for expecting such results.

When I took charge of my present school, I found neither the boarding-house nor school-building provided with any proper modes of ventilation, and after making all changes for improvement at command, it is still needful to make it the constant duty of one teacher to see that, so far as practicable, every room in school and boarding-house is properly warmed and ventilated every hour of the day and night.

In regard to the course of study in the collegiate department of a woman's university, there should be as great an amount as is required in any of our colleges, yet only a few studies carried to so great an extent as in many sciences pursued by men. But there should be a much *greater variety*, together with an accuracy and thoroughness that colleges rarely secure. And all should have reference to women's profession, and not to the professions of men. Much in this department at first must be experimental, having in view the ideal indicated.

So in regard to introducing *practical* training for woman's domestic duties *as a part of common school education*; although it is certain that much more can be done than ever has been attempted, and that, too, as a contribution to intellectual development rather than the reverse, this also must be a matter of experiment.

In regard to a *special* training in the preparatory and the collegiate schools for future self-supporting employments, much more can be done than has ever been supposed, and a few particulars will be enumerated to illustrate. Young women of affectionate disposition, good intelligence and morals, having only limited means, might be trained to become a *mother's assistant* in charge of a nursery, partly by the studies of the primary and preparatory schools and partly by learning the methods of the Kindergarten. Thousands of parents in all parts of our nation would offer liberal wages to young women thus trained for one of the most sacred offices of the family state.

Women of suitable social and moral character might be trained, *in connection with school studies*, to be superior seamstresses and mantua-makers, and thus be enabled to gain liberal wages.

If young ladies knew how much usefulness and comfort may be connected with this domestic art, they would seek it with more interest than any school study. The scarcity of well-trained mantua-makers in all parts of the land has made my early training in this art a great blessing to me and to many others whom I have been thus enabled to aid and to teach; and there is no branch of school training that can be made so directly available in promoting economy, comfort, and usefulness.

Women trained to fit young boys for college, in private families or in small neighborhood schools, would command very high remuneration in many quarters. *Every* young girl whose means will allow it ought to be prepared for this duty.

Pupils who have a decided talent for either music, drawing, or other fine arts, might have a *special* training for one of these professions; while those without any such tastes or aptitudes should be dissuaded from wasting time, labor, and money, as is so absurdly and widely practiced, in learning to play the piano and acquiring other accomplishments never pursued in after-life. Nine tenths of young girls thus instructed lose all they learn in a very short period.

Some pupils have fine voices and a talent and taste for elocution, and such might be trained for teachers of this art or for public readings.

Some pupils have talents that prepare them to excel in authorship, and to such an appropriate and more extensive literary culture could be afforded.

The art of book-keeping and of quick and legible penmanship insures remunerative employment; and many other specialties might be enumerated in which, *during school-days*, a woman might be trained to a self-supporting profession. And *every* woman should be trained for all the duties that may in future life be demanded as wife, mother, nurse, and school-teacher, if not in the ordinary school, in a separate professional school.

When institutions are endowed to train women for all departments connected with the family state, domestic labor, now so shunned and disgraced, will become honorable, will gain liberal compensation, and will enable every woman to secure an independence in employments suited to her sex. And when this is attained, there will be few or none who will wish to enter the professions of men or take charge of civil government.

Having expressed so strongly my views in reference to large boarding-schools for both sexes, I will add some further details of my *ideal* for organizing a Woman's University. This has been suggested by recent interviews with some who may have much influence in managing the large funds recently bequeathed in Massachusetts for establishing institutions for women, in one case a lady having bestowed what will probably amount to nearly half a million, and in another case a gentleman has bequeathed a million and a half for this purpose.

This, I believe, is but the beginning of similar benefactions that will be provided for women in all parts of our country. There are men of wealth who have lost a dear mother, wife, or daughter, who would find comfort and pleasure in perpetuating a beloved name by an endowment that for age after age will minister to the education and refinement of women and the support and training of orphans.

In this view, it seems very important that the first endowed institutions of this kind should adopt plans that may be wisely imitated.

It seems desirable that such endowed institutions should be placed in or so near a large town that the pupils of all the schools, except the professional one, should reside with their parents instead of congregating in a great boarding-house. The professional school would ordinarily embrace only women of maturity, and might demand a location with surrounding land for floriculture, horticulture, and other feminine professions.

The Kindergarten, the primary school, and the preparatory school might each have a principal and an associate principal, supported partly by tuition fees and partly by endowment. These principals might establish a family, consisting of the two, who would take the place of parents to several adopted orphans and to several pay-pupils whose parents, from ill health or other causes, would relinquish the care of their children.

The collegiate schools might have endowed departments corresponding to professorships in colleges, each having a principal and associate principal, who also could establish families on the same plan. When completed, the university would then consist of a central building for school purposes, surrounded by fifteen or twenty families, each having a principal and associate principal, acting as parents to a family of from ten to twelve pupils, and all in some department of domestic training.

Thus some thirty or forty ladies of high character and culture would be provided with the independence and advantages now exclusively bestowed on men, while at the same time the institution would practically and to a considerable extent be an orphan asylum offering unusual advantages.

In regard to the practicability of finding women properly qualified to carry on such a university with success, there is no difficulty. Few know so well as I do how many women of benevolence and high culture are living with half their noblest energies unemployed for want of the opportunities and facilities provided for men. There is nothing needed but *endowments* to secure the services of a large number of ladies of the highest culture and moral worth, well qualified to establish not only one but many such institutions.

In my attempts to organize female institutions on the college plan of independent principals of endowed departments, responsible not to an individual but to a faculty and corporation, I have been met with objections that apply as much to colleges for men. The jealousies and jars incident to all complex institutions are the result of the frailties of humanity common to both sexes. I have, in a large number of instances, organized institutions on the college plan, which for years were conducted with perfect harmony, some of them are still prospering, and others were ended only for want of endowments to retain the highest class of teachers.

An Address to Ladies of Hartford, Conn.,

Invited from all Religious Denominations; Delivered at the Calisthenic Hall of the Hartford Female Seminary, May, 1871.

Ladies and Kind Friends:

At a former meeting I stated that, as former principal of this Seminary, I so exhausted my nervous system that I have never been able to assume responsibilities involving obligations which, by my failure, would cause disappointment to others. My method, therefore, has been to originate plans, and then induce others, more capable than myself, to execute them, and in such a way that I could help without taking any responsibility.

Thus I originated the plan for transferring teachers to the West, executed by Gov. Slade. And thus also I organized the American Women's Educational Association, for securing *endowed* collegiate and professional schools for women, which has established several flourishing institutions at the West. The most important of these is the Milwaukee Female College, which for more than fifteen years has been conducted by the chief agent of this Association, Miss Mary Mortimer; and which now numbers 180 pupils, and exhibits many of the benefits of our plan, although only partially endowed. The object of this meeting is to gain your influence in order to secure, not only what has been gained at Milwaukee, but to accomplish the whole plan of a fully endowed Woman's University, as the model which we hope to see reproduced all over the nation.

In all these educational efforts, I have been led by a deep and painful sense of the depressed and suffering condition of large portions of our sex, and to an extent little realized by women in easy and prosperous circumstances. I introduce here an extract from a published article of mine that gives some small exhibition of these painful facts.

> That there is something essentially wrong in the present condition of women, is every year growing more and more apparent, while the public mind is more and more perplexed with diverse

methods proposed for the remedy. In one of our leading secular papers we read this statement of the case from the pen of a working woman:

> "There are so few departments of labor open to women, that, in those departments, the supply of female labor is frightfully in advance of the demand. The business world offers the lowest wages to eager applicants, certain that they will be ravenously clutched. And, indeed, to see the mob of women that block and choke these few and narrow gates open to them—the struggle—the press—the agony—the trembling eagerness—you might suppose they were entering the temple of fame or wealth, or, at least had some cosy little cottage ahead, in which competence awaited the winner. Nothing of the sort. These are blind alleys, one and all. The mere getting in, and keeping in, are the meagre objects of this terrible struggle. A woman who has not *genius,* or is not a *rare exception,* has no opening—no promotion—no career. She turns hopelessly on a pivot; at every turn the sand gives way, and she sinks lower. At every turn light and air are more difficult, and she turns and digs her own grave. Do you say these are figures of speech? Here, then, are figures of *fact*. There are *now thirty thousand* women in New York, whose labor averages from *twelve to fifteen hours a day*, and yet whose income seldom exceeds *thirty-three cents a day*. Operators on sewing-machines, and a few others, enjoy comparative opulence, gaining five to eight dollars a week, though from this are to be paid three or four dollars for a bed in a wretched room with several other occupants, often without a window or any provision for pure air, and with only the poor food found where such rooms abound. Thousands of ladies, of good family and education, as teachers receive from two to six hundred dollars a year. Few women get beyond that, and a large proportion of them are mothers with children. Over these poorly-paid laborers broods the sense of hopeless toil. There is no bright future. The woman who is fevered, hurried, and aching, who works from daylight to midnight, loathing her mean room, her meaner dress, her joyless life, will, in ten years, neither better herself nor her children. The American working-woman has no share in the American privilege given to the poorest *male* laborer—a growing income, a bank account, and every office of the Republic, if he have brain and courage to win them."

This describes the condition and feelings of not all, but of a large class of women in many of our larger cities, who must earn their own livelihood. But, in the medium classes, as it respects wealth, the unmarried or widowed women feel that they are an incumbrance to fathers and brothers, who often unwillingly support them from pride or duty. For such, also, there is "no opening—no promotion—no career;" and they must remain dependent chiefly on the labor of others till marriage is offered, which to vast numbers is a positive impossibility.

This has lately been proved, from the census, by a leading New York paper. In that it is shown that, in all our large cities, the male inhabitants, under fifteen and over the usual marriageable age, are greatly in excess of the females, and, consequently, the women at the marriageable age are greatly in excess of the marriageable men. Thus, in New York City, according to the statements of the *New York Times*, there are eleven thousand more females than males, of all ages, while there are one hundred and thirty-two thousand more women of marriageable age than men of that age. This is perhaps a large estimate, but the disproportion is at all events enormous.

And, in the rural districts of New York State, we find a similar state of things; for the excess of females, of all ages, is twenty-one thousand, while the excess of marriageable women, if at the same ratio as that stated in New York City, would be two hundred and sixty-three thousand. A similar state of things will be seen in all our older States.

The most mournful feature in this case is the fact that most of these women have never been trained for any kind of business by which they can earn an independent livelihood. The Working-woman's Protective Union, of New York City, reports that, of thirteen thousand applicants, not one-half were qualified to do any kind of useful work in a proper manner. The societies that are formed to furnish work for poor women report that their greatest impediment is that so few can sew decently, or do any other work properly.

The heads of dress-making establishments report that very few women can be found who can be trusted to complete a dress, and that those who are competent find abundant work and good wages. The demand for really superior mantua-makers is almost universal in country places, and even in many of our cities.

In former days sewing was taught in all schools for girls, but now it is banished from our common schools, and the mothers at home are too neglectful, or too ignorant, or too pressed with labor, to supply the deficiency.

It was reported in the *New York Tribune*, not long since, that there are at least twenty thousand professed prostitutes in New York City alone, while Boston, in proportion to its number of inhabitants, shows a larger number, and all our cities give similar reports. This, it is hoped is an estimate much in excess of the reality; but the truth is mournful enough. Multitudes of these unfortunates have only two alternatives—on the one hand, poor lodgings, shabby dress, poor food, and ceaseless daily toil from eight to ten or fifteen hours; on the other hand, the tempter offers a pleasant home, a servant to do the work, fine dress, the theatre and ball, and kind attentions, with no labor or care. Where is the strength of virtue in those who despise and avoid these outcasts, that might not fall in such perilous assaults?

It is this dreadful state of temptation which accounts for the fact that crime increases faster among women than among men. Thus, in Massachusetts, during the last ten years, among the men of that State, crime *decreased* at the rate of eight thousand five hundred and seven less than during the ten preceding years, while, among women, crime *increased* at the rate of three hundred and sixty-eight during the same period; that is, over eight thousand *less* men, and over three hundred *more* women, were guilty of crime than in the previous ten years.

But, turning from these to the daughters of the most wealthy class, those who have generous and elevated aspirations also feel that for them, too, there is "no opening—no promotion—no career," except that of marriage, and for this they are trained to feel that it is disgraceful to seek. They have nothing to do but wait to be sought. Trained to believe marriage their highest boon, they are disgraced for seeking it, and must affect indifference.

Meantime, to do any thing to earn their own independence is what father and brothers would deem a disgrace to themselves and their family. For women of high position to work for their livelihood, in most cases custom decrees as disgraceful. And then, if cast down by poverty, they have been trained to nothing that would earn a support, or, if by chance they have some resource, all avenues for its employment are thronged with needy applicants. Ordinarily, and with few exceptions, there are only two employments for such women that do not involve loss of social position, viz., school-teaching and boarding.

But every opening for a school-teacher has scores, and sometimes hundreds, of applicants, while often the protracted toils in unventilated and crowded school rooms destroy health. To keep boarders demands capital to start, and an experience and training in household management and economy rarely taught to the daughters of wealth. In this country housework is dishonorable, and rich men make no attempts to train their daughters to any other business that would be a resort in poverty.

Few can realize the perils which threaten our country from the present condition of women. The grand instrumentality, not only for perpetuating our race, but for its training to eternal blessedness, is the family state, and in this woman is the chief minister. As the general rule, man is the laborer out of the home, to provide for its support, while woman is the daily minister to train its inmates. But there are now many fatal influences that combine to unfit her for these sacred duties. Not the least of these is the decay of female health, engendering irritable nerves in both mother and offspring, and thus greatly increasing the difficulties of physical and still more of moral training.

The factory girls, and many also in shops and stores, must stand eight and ten hours a day, often in a poisonous atmosphere, causing decay of constitution, and forbidding healthful offspring. The sewing-machine lessens the wages of needlewomen, while employers testify that those who use it for steady work become hopelessly diseased, and cannot rear healthy children. In the more wealthy circles, the murderous fashions of dress make terrible havoc with the health of young girls, while impure air, unhealthful food and condiments, lack of exercise, and over-stimulation of brain and nerves, are completing the ruin of health and family hopes.

The state of domestic service is another element that is undermining the family state. Disgraced by the stigma of our late slavery, and by the influx into our kitchens of ignorant and uncleanly foreigners, American women forsake home circles for the unhealthful shops and mills.

Then the thriftless young housekeepers from boarding-school life have no ability either to teach or to control their incompetent assistants, while ceaseless "worries" multiply in parlor, nursery, and kitchen. The husband is discouraged by the waste and extravagance, and wearied with endless complaints, and home becomes any thing but the harbor of comfort and peace.

Add to all this, the now common practice which destroys maternal health and unborn offspring—the loose teachings of free love—the unfortunate influence of spiritualism, so called—the fascinations of the *demi-monde* for the rich, and of lower haunts for the rest, with the poverty of thousands of women who but for desperate temptations would be pure, and the extent of the malign influences undermining the family state—that chief hope of our race—is appalling.

Woman, in the Protestant world, is educated only *for marriage,* hoping to have some one to work for her support, and, when this is not gained, little else is provided.

The Roman Catholic Church, while it honored the institution of marriage as a sacrament, and upheld its sanctity, yet taught that woman had a still higher ministry; and for this, large endowments, comfortable positions, and honorable distinction, were provided. The women who devoted their time and wealth and labors to orphans, to the sick, and to the poor, were honored above married women as *saints,* who not only laid up treasures in heaven for themselves, but also a stock of *merits* to supply the deficiencies of others. The idea of self-sacrifice and self-denial in that church was so honored as to run into mischievous extremes, so that rich establishments of celibates of both sexes multiplied all over Christendom till they became burdens and pests.

This drove the Protestant world to the other extreme, so that no provision at all has been made for the single woman. In most cases she must marry, or have no profession that leads to independence, honor, and wealth. To fit young men for their professions, thousands and millions are every year provided, securing by endowments the highest class of teachers, in addition to every advantage of libraries, apparatus, and buildings. But woman's profession has no such provisions made for its elevated duties.

In the Roman Catholic Church the woman of high position, culture, and benevolence, is honored above all others if she remains single and devotes her time and wealth to orphans, to nurse the sick, to reclaim the vicious, and to provide for the destitute. She becomes a lady abbess, or the head of some sisterhood, where high position, influence, and honor, are her reward.

And the priesthood of that Church employ all their personal and official influence to lead women of benevolence and piety to devote time, property, and prayers, to the salvation of their fellow-creatures from diseases of body, ignorance, and sin.

But Protestant women, as yet, have been influenced to endow institutions for *men,* rather than for their own sex. The writer obtained from the treasurers of only six institutions for men the following statement of benefactions from women:

Miss Plummer, to Cambridge University, to endow one professorship, gave $25,000; Mary Townsend, for the same, $25,000; Sarah Jackson, for the same, $10,000; other ladies, in sums over $1,000, to the same, over $30,000. To Andover Professional School of Theology ladies have given over $65,000, and, of this, $30,000

> by one lady. In Illinois, Mrs. Garretson has given to one professional school $300,000. In Albany, Mrs. Dudlay has given, for a scientific institution for men, $105,000. To Beloit College, Wisconsin, property has been given, by one lady, valued at $30,000.
>
> Thus half a million has been given by women to these six colleges and professional schools, and all in the present century. The reports of similar institutions for men all over the nation would show similar liberal benefactions of women to endow institutions for the other sex, while for their own no such records appear. Where is there a single endowment from a woman to secure a salary to a woman teaching her own proper profession?

It is the depressed and suffering condition of our sex, here indicated, which is the exciting cause of the agitation to gain woman suffrage. To me, success in this effort appears not as a remedy, but rather as a curse. But there are favorable results involved in this agitation that deserve consideration. One is, the exhibition of the moral power now held by women in our nation. For if women urging measures so contrary to our customs and prejudices—not to say so contrary to common sense and the Bible—with many prominent leaders so destitute of discretion and political foresight, yet can move society so powerfully, what could not be accomplished by the organized influence and action of that vast majority of intelligent women opposed to such innovations?

Another beneficial result it is hoped will be, systematic and concerted measures by judicious and benevolent women to organize agencies to remedy the evils all must lament, and by measures more wise and more practicable. What such measure will probably be, may be indicated by a series of resolutions adopted first by two previous meetings, and afterwards by a large public meeting at Steinway Hall, New York, of ladies invited by the Managers of the American Woman's Educational Association, from all religious denominations in the city, as follows:

> "Resolved, That one cause of the depressed condition of woman is the fact that the distinctive profession of her sex, as the nurse of infancy and of the sick, as educator of childhood, and as the chief minister of the family state, has not been duly honored, nor such provision been made for its scientific and practical training as is accorded to the other sex for their professions; and, that it is owing to this neglect that women are driven to seek honor and independence in the institutions and the professions of men.
>
> "Resolved, That woman's distinctive profession, in its various branches, involves more important interests than any other human science; and, that the evils suffered by women would be extensively remedied by establishing institutions for training women for her profession, which shall be as generously endowed as are the institutions of men, many of which have been largely endowed by women.

"Resolved, That the science of domestic economy should be made a study in all institutions for girls; and that certain practical employments of the family state should be made a part of common school education, especially the art of sewing, which is so needful for the poor.

"Resolved, That every young woman should be trained to some business by which she can earn an independent livelihood in case of poverty.

"Resolved, That in addition to the various in-door employments suitable for woman, there are other out-door employments especially favorable to health and equally suitable, such as raising fruits and flowers, the culture of silk and cotton, the raising of bees, and the superintendence of dairy farms and manufactures. All of these offer avenues to wealth and independence for women as properly as men, and schools for imparting to women the science and practice of these employments should be provided, and as liberally endowed as are the agricultural schools for men." These resolutions were adopted unanimously and then published in all the leading secular and religious papers with equally unanimous approval. The following from the *N. Y. Evening Post,* is a fair specimen of the whole.

"These resolutions contain sound sense; and their claim that practical schools for women deserve as much attention as similar schools for men, is undeniably just. If we are to have industrial schools at all, if it is important that anybody should be able to secure systematic and thorough instruction as a preparation for useful industries, girls would be as much benefited by such instruction as boys; and women need it as much as men.

"There is no doubt that the present arrangement of society bears more hardly upon women than upon men; and all wise efforts to make them more independent of the mischances of life deserve encouragement."

Although the plan aimed at is large, this Association commenced with only a small portion. At Milwaukee, where is their first institution, a school already organized was taken as the nucleus. The citizens were to furnish land, and building, and pupils enough to support by tuition fees a given number of teachers. On these conditions the Association agreed to provide endowments to support a certain number of teachers, so long as the plan of the Association was carried out, but if it was relinquished, to remove their patronage to another place. The Lady Agent of the Association is still at the head of this Institution, which has prospered on this plan for more than fifteen years, the Association supporting by their funds a portion of the teachers.

In my former address in this place, I showed how in this and other cities, the more wealthy, and best educated classes, and those who pay the most taxes for public education, provide for their own daughters inferior advantages to those given to the humblest poor. Our own High School in this city compared with this Seminary and all private schools, will illustrate this remarkable fact.

For our High School has a building healthfully and thoroughly warmed and ventilated, as can be said of neither this Seminary, nor any private school of this city; while its apparatus and library are superior to any except those of the College, and the Theological School, to which no girls have access. By reason of subordinate graded schools, only well prepared pupils are admitted, or this is the rule which can be enforced; while all scholars must enter at regular periods. Thus, only four classes are formed and only a small number of studies are pursued at any one time. The teachers are thus allowed time to prepare themselves, and other great advantages for instructing, while their salaries are much higher than can be given to assistant teachers in most private schools. Thus the best class of teachers are tempted to forsake private schools for these superior advantages.

In contrast to these advantages, although this Seminary is warmed and ventilated as well as most private schools, it is necessary to employ much of the time of an intelligent and careful teacher to keep the rooms at proper temperature, well ventilated and free from poisonous gases, and yet with but imperfect success.

Then the pupils enter this and all private schools, at any time and at all grades of advancement, making it necessary to multiply classes and to tax the teachers in order to bring forward the new comers to certain classes. The method of arranging certain studies at one time of the year, and others only at other times, as in colleges and our public high schools, often cannot be enforced without dissatisfying patrons, and thus lessening income. Then the accomplishments, especially Piano music, to which classes must conform, greatly increases the difficulty of classification in this and in all private schools.

The result usually is, a most inferior, desultory, and unsatisfactory course of education. There are cases where by overworking poorly paid assistant teachers, and by small profits to proprietors, some private schools turn out as fine scholars as our best managed High schools. But these are exceptions, and exceptions that bear very severely on the subordinate women teachers.

Thus comes to pass the remarkable fact that the most wealthy and cultivated pay the largest taxes to furnish the poorer classes a gratuitous and a better education than they gain for their own daughters by paying the largest tuition fees, or at expensive boarding schools.

There is great misconception as to the advantages of education for daughters of the more wealthy classes, owing to the fact that the ambitious name of "college" is given to schools that have no proper claim to this appellation. For the distinctive feature of a college heretofore has been its *endowments*, by which a permanent faculty of superior and co-equal teachers are maintained to a great extent independent of tuition fees; and also supporting professors as independent heads of departments, instead of subordinates to a principal, as in High Schools and academies. This being the fact, there is not a single college for women in this country, nor in the whole world.

The only feature of a college in any institutions for women is a similar course of study and graduating diplomas, and these without endowments only increase the branches taught, and decrease the thoroughness of instruction and overwork the teachers.

There is also great misconception as to the influence of woman's domestic duties in developing and training the intellect. A problem in arithmetic or geometry is far more interesting, and therefore more quickening to the intellect, when it is directly applied to some useful, practical purpose. Thus a woman who is daily calculating her butcher's and grocer's accounts, or trading at stores, is cultivating her intellect as much or more than she would by studying arithmetic in college or school without any end but to escape reproof or marks of imperfection. So the planning and cutting garments and the various other calculations and measurements of carpets, curtains, and furniture, are daily exercises in both geometry and arithmetic, while the practical interest and the handicraft involved tend to quicken intellectual vigor.

Then in kitchen affairs, domestic chemistry, though on a small scale, is constantly studied and practically applied. Again in the care of infants and of the sick, the discipline of the physiologist and the physician are united. Then in the government of servants and children, the same mental exertion and principles are employed as are demanded for legislatures, statesmen, and magistrates. Then in the religious training of children, all the most profound questions of the metaphysician and the theologian are daily objects of enquiry and reflection as childhood urges the most difficult problems of mental science, and of natural and revealed religion.

A man in his daily toils, or in the learned professions has only one or two subjects that hold his practical attention and interest, but a woman as mother and housekeeper has a constant succession of employments that tax all her intellectual and her moral powers. These views are remarkably illustrated by some of the women of a former generation whose intellectual training was chiefly in domestic pursuits with little else except the humblest kind of common school, a very small library, and a vigorous pulpit ministry. Let such be compared with multitudes of women who with little domestic training and exercise have graduated from the High Schools and Colleges of the present day, and we shall have occasion for serious reflection as to the diverse results.

I can best illustrate this by an individual case that may fairly represent a large class of women forty or fifty years ago. In early youth I lived in Litchfield, Conn., where a law school was conducted by Judge Reeves, and Judge Gould, two of the most talented and learned jurists of the nation, and gathered from forty to over one hundred law students from the first colleges and the first families of every state in the Union. There were also eight or ten other gentlemen of liberal education and some of more than ordinary talents and culture, in the same circle.

Then of the ladies I met in that circle, were Mrs. Judge Reeve, Mrs. Judge Gould, Miss Sarah Pierce, to whom I owe my school education, Miss Mary Pierce, Miss Amelia Ogden, Miss Lucy Sheldon, my father's sister Esther, my mother's sister Mrs. Mary Hubbard, and my mother. In my own family circle I used to hear my mother and aunts discussing a variety of literary and scientific topics, and especially remember their enthusiastic interest in the new discoveries of chemistry by Lavoisier, and their practical test experiments in the kitchen and study. Aunt Esther was deeply interested in medical science, and probably had read medical works as extensively as most physicians of that day.

Then Mrs. Judge Reeve, and my mother and aunts, would meet and read works of history, or travels, or some classic English literature. Miss Mary Pierce was an accomplished elocutionist, and when Judge Gould suffered from weak eyes, would go day after day to read works of literature and discuss the topics introduced. Miss Sarah Pierce was head of the largest and most celebrated female school of the nation, and was overflowing with acquired knowledge, as well as poetic treasures.

Now not one of these ladies had studied a line of Latin or Greek, or of mathematics or other college studies which women are now seeking so earnestly at the sacrifice of health and all domestic culture. And yet when they met these gentlemen of the highest talents and education, they were regarded as fully their equals in mental power and intellectual debate. Indeed, some of my brothers educated in this circle, honestly maintained that women were endowed by nature with intellectual powers superior to men; and one brother argued in defence of this position in a public college exercise. Moreover, six brothers had a college education, while none of my sisters studied any part of the college course; and yet there has been no marked inequality of mental power and culture in this diverse training.

In that day, novels, by most women, were either deemed an unlawful indulgence, or were taken as condiments only, while the substantials of literature and science were their chief intellectual pabulum. And having but few books and those the choice works of the best English classics, they were perused and reperused with such interest as rarely is given in colleges to the literature of Greece and Rome. And it was a frequent fact, that women were far better read in English classic literature than were their brothers and friends in colleges.

Now at the present day, when mothers and housekeepers meet gentlemen in social gatherings, is there anything in their conversation and pursuits to show the superior advantages of the female High Schools and Colleges, which have nearly supplanted the intellectual domestic training of a former generation? Have not novels, magazine stories, newspaper literature, and the fashions and accomplishments of the age taken the place of the more vigorous mental culture so common at a former period?

A variety of intellectual training which is pursued in connection with such interesting practical results as woman's employments involve, tends to produce a vigorous and well balanced mind, far more than devotion to one or two professional pursuits such as the business of most men requires. And even in science and literature, we not unfrequently find some of the most learned men entirely deficient in intellectual balance and executive power; while their less learned mothers or wives are respected as wise and practical counselors.

The diminution of domestic exercise in the family state by mothers and daughters has equally tended to the loss of physical development and vigor in the present generation of women. The Creator has wisely adapted the physical organization of woman to her appropriate duties, so that the alternating sedentary and active exercises of the nursery and household are exactly those best fitted to sustain and invigorate the organs which now are so extensively displaced or diseased. And the artificial modes of exercise to remedy these evils, now so successful in the Movement Cure, are to a large extent in imitation of these domestic muscular movements demanded in the nursery and in other household labors. The tending of infants, the bending, twisting, and stooping constantly practiced in these domestic labors are exactly what are demanded to preserve in health and activity the muscles most important to womanly development and vigor; while the interchanging employment of the needle and other sedentary domestic pursuits, when in proper proportion, equally tend to healthful results. Very different are the influences on woman's health as she stands six and eight hours behind the counter or in shops and mills in one continuous and unvaried toil, or sits day after day over the needle without intervening healthful exercises. Not less are the evils to the daughters of wealth and ease, whose brain and nerves are never relieved and strengthened by the exercises of domestic life. Still more lamentable is the common practice of those who, when sending daughters to the public schools, free them from domestic labor, that they may give their whole time to study and school duties. If instead of this, these pupils were required to engage in domestic labor two hours each day and this amount of time was deducted from school duties, not only health but higher intellectual development would be secured.

If a time should come when the aims of the Woman Suffrage party are attained, and women are trained for the pulpit, the bar, the political arena, and other professions drawing woman from domestic life, still more disastrous influences will show the great mistake of taking woman from her true sphere and giving her the work designed for man. If, on the contrary, women are trained to both the science and the practice of their true profession in all its varied departments, and with the honor and emolument that now are given exclusively to the professions of men, every woman will be in demand for the services of the family and the school, and will regard the employments of men as less important and less inviting than her own sacred ministries.

It is often said that it is mothers who must give the domestic training to daughters, and that school duties should be confined to literature and science. This might have been true in former days, when daughters and mothers performed most of the family labor, and when the style of living was simple and economical. But with the present style of houses and expenditures, demanding two, three or more servants, it is utterly impossible for a mother and housekeeper to add to her multiplied cares the scientific domestic training of her daughters; nor can anything of this kind be successfully connected with large boarding schools. The demand for *scientific* domestic training is greatly increased by improved modern conveniences.

The one item of selecting and superintending the management of stoves and furnaces, demands much scientific study and practical instruction, and there is no one point where family health and economy suffer more than for want of them. The inhaling of poisonous gases, the sudden changes of temperature, and the want of proper ventilation probably are doing more to destroy the constitution and health of families than any other cause, and owing greatly to the want of needed science and skill in housekeepers.

In various other departments, the increase of civilization and its elegancies and conveniences have greatly increased the need of scientific training for mothers and housekeepers, who, never having been thus instructed themselves, are not qualified to train their daughters.

As to the virtue of economy, in our nation among the more wealthy classes, it seems to have become one of "the lost arts." The art and skill of domestic economy can no more be acquired without instruction and training, than any of the mechanical trades. As eldest daughter of a poor minister, and the pupil of a most ingenious mother and a vigorously economical aunt, I know that by proper training, a young lady can dress with taste and propriety at one half the expense required by one untrained; and that a housekeeper without such a preparation needs double the means of one who is properly instructed. Not that there are not women as well as men, who have natural gifts that enable them to excel in handicraft and skill without any training, so as to equal those properly instructed. But these are exceptional cases.

To illustrate the fact that the more civilization increases the enjoyments and refinements of the family state, the more it multiplies the responsibilities and cares of a mother and housekeeper, I will reproduce a specimen of such conversations as I have repeatedly had with familiar friends. The lady introduced, is a mother of five young children all attending some primary, or some higher schools, and in reply to her remark that she had no time for solid or systematic reading, I enquired,

"How many servants have you?"

"Three; a cook, a chambermaid, and a boy for errands and care of yard and garden."

"Now suppose," said I, "that you give me an outline of your ordinary daily routine, that I may appreciate your difficulties; for I think few understand how much is demanded of mother and housekeeper in these days. At what hour do you rise?"

"Usually about seven; and then beside dressing myself, I must see that the little ones are washed and dressed properly, as all the servants are busy. Their hair must be combed and braided, their teeth and nails in order, and their clothing be all whole and clean for school, which often demands an extra stitch, or some change that I must regulate. This takes till near breakfast hour, when I go down to see that all is right on the table and in the kitchen. When I have a good cook, and second girl, I have not much to do; but the frequent changes oblige me often to be training, or overseeing one or the other. Then at table, I serve the tea and coffee, and also take care of the two youngest, to supply proper food, and see that they behave properly."

"Cannot your husband take some of this care."

"Oh, no; he is so hurried in business and so anxious to get off as soon as possible.

"Then we have prayers, and I must collect all the family, and see that all the children behave properly. Then I make a memorandum of errands or purchases for my husband to execute. Then I must see that all the children are prepared for school, their books all collected, their hair dressed, and shoes in order, and all their little wants supplied.

"Then I go to the kitchen and make arrangements with the cook for the day, giving written orders for the grocer and butcher. Then I arrange the work for the second girl for the day. I go over all the rooms and chambers myself, and always find in my drawers and closets something that needs care or labor, that I must do myself, or arrange for others to do. Oh, the making, the mending, the altering, the washing, and the care of clothing for young children which our present fashions require! And yet I always hang back and do as little as possible without being odd, or making the children fear lest all their companions should outdo them.

"By noon I am so tired and nervous I can not do anything more than sit down quietly and look over the morning paper. Then comes the noon lunch, when I again have all the table serving and care of children. After lunch, I send out the children to play, and then comes the family sewing and mending, the shopping—to buy dresses, bonnets, shoes, gloves, trimmings, and all the numerous et ceteras of the wardrobe for husband, children, and self. The mantua-maker must come some days, and then what worry and work! Then the sempstress comes other times; then company calls that I must entertain; and then comes the children's music practice, and their hard lessons in arithmetic or geometry, where I must help or oversee.

"Then comes the dinner at 5 or 6, when company often is added, and I must see that all is in order, and the children well behaved, and the table served aright. For an hour or two after dinner comes a little time to talk with my husband and children; but again I am called on to help in the lessons of the older children, or to aid them when sewing or drawing. Then I must go to prepare the little ones for bed, as both servants are busy after dinner.

"All this is what I do when I have no visitors, and when there is no baby. But when there is a nurse and a baby, and visitors staying in the family to entertain, I am sure I do not know how I get through all. I only know that most of my married life I have suffered constant weariness, and a pain in head or back, and that all put together make life such a burden that often I should willingly lay it down were it not for my dear husband and children.

"And all these beautiful things around me, and my lovely home, seem to double my cares because I have so much to keep in order. For all these rich and delicate things are soon ruined if left in the hands of servants, and the more we get, the more we have to watch and work to save from injury or waste."

"If we lived in such a convenient little cottage as you have put in your American Woman's Home, and had a highly educated governess, and then all of us united to do the family work, except washing and ironing, how much easier and happier life would be!"[2]

But at present my thoughts and efforts are most engaged to accomplish that department of a Women's University which relates to the preservation and restoration of health. When often asked what is the reason that our women are so delicate and unhealthy, and that our young girls so often suffer what in former days was rare and then only in connexion with maternity, my reply often is, that it is because parents and teachers are doing every thing they can do to produce such mischiefs.

Sleeping in unventilated chambers; living in schoolrooms and parlors heated to excess and charged with poisonous gases; exposed to sudden variations of temperature from mismanagement; eating unhealthful food at irregular hours and to a dangerous excess; supplied with unhealthful confectionery to eat at any hour; indulged in exciting amusements with late hours for sleep; the brain stimulated by a multitude of school duties and studies unrelieved by muscular exercises; the dress contrived to impede vital functions, compressing the most yielding parts so as to force the upper organs on to the lower, generating the most cruel displacements and mental and bodily diseases; over-heating the parts most injured by such treatment, and exposing the parts most important to keep warm; compressing feet and ankles so as to impede circulation, with high heels throwing all the muscles out of natural play so as to increase all the dangerous tendencies to internal displacement; these are only one portion of the many contrivances adopted or allowed by parents and teachers to destroy the health of women and young girls.

The public press is now circulating such charges against the most cultivated Protestant women of our country as, if true, will verify the assertion that in one important respect, "Protestantism is a failure." For maternity in its normal aspect, involves what scripture represents as the extremity of physical suffering. If to this

[2] This book is enlarged and has questions for a text book for schools. Its title is "Principles of Domestic Science," and it is published by J. B. Ford, Park Place, New York. The second part entitled The House Keeper & Health Keeper is in press and will be published in the fall by the Harpers.

is added the protracted tortures of mind and body consequent on such outrages on nature as are narrated above, it is not the graduates of boarding schools, and High Schools and Colleges who are to be the mothers and educators of this nation, but those rather who are protected from these sins and sufferings by humble means, daily toil, and a vigilant and politic priesthood.

All through my early days, no such charges against womanhood were even imagined, for I saw a cheerful, healthful mother each second or third year of her whole married life with another healthful infant, and all received by my father as a precious "heritage from the Lord" and through his long life his "chief joy and crown of rejoicing." And this, which is now so rare an example, was a common experience, in that more simple and healthful generation.

My opportunities for noticing the decline of health in women of this generation, and forming opinions on medical subjects, have been extensive, as for over forty years I have been taxing the science and sagacity of medical men in all parts of the nation, residing in many health establishments, reading medical works, and consulting all classes of medical practitioners. In this course I have secured perfect health and also learned many lessons that I hope will enable me to aid others in gaining the same blessing.

And the most important of these lessons is, that most diseases are consequences of violating the laws of health, (which are as really the laws of God as any in the Bible), and that the surest and safest remedies are found in conforming to these laws. This will be illustrated by a short account of my experiences while so long a wandering invalid.

During this period, as results have proved, I had no organic or functional disease, except extreme prostration of the overworked brain and nerves, increased by a punctured nerve, adding to the debility of the connected sciatic nerve. Thus came inability to walk without supporters, and little ability for any kind of either mental or physical exercise.

The treatment to be narrated was in all cases but one, by regularly educated physicians, most of whom were regarded as among the highest in talents and skill, often the professors of medical colleges. The first physician prescribed a heaping teaspoonful of carbonate of iron three times a day, which was taken with no benefit. Next, a learned professor, for a slight fever bled twice, and, to allay consequent nervous excitement, gave camphor till temporary deafness ensued. Next, another medical professor conjectured that the lameness resulted from the state of the stomach, and gave small doses of rheubarb three times a day with no advantage. Then another considered the spine as the diseased point, and applied irritating ointments. Another prescribed galvanism, but could give no rule as to time or manner, or expected effects, but hoped that somehow it might do some good. Several prescribed local applications to the limb, which in all cases increased the difficulty.

These all failing, I commenced my rounds to health establishments. The first was conducted by a sagacious and learned German physician, who conjectured that the cause of the lameness was the state of the blood, and used cold water to produce a skin eruption which came without any good result. But during a year's residence there, I saw most remarkable cures of many diseases, by treating the skin with alternations of heat and cold connected with simple food, and outdoor exercise. In repeated cases I saw thin, pale victims of tubercular consumption, some apparently in the last stages, changed to rosy, plump and vigorous women by this treatment. Here I also gained in vigor of mind and body, though under the most heroic water treatment, but the weak limb was unrelieved.

Then I resorted to an establishment where the treatment was confined to simple food, only one or two articles being allowed at one meal. To this was added short gymnastic exercises, alternating with short periods of rest. Here I found that by reducing the quantity of food, and taking only one or two articles at a meal I gained both in flesh and strength, but the weak limb prevented the required exercises and was unrelieved.

Then resort was had to an establishment where many women were cured of internal displacements and consequent evils, but a lady physician by proper investigation, decided that my lameness resulted from no such cause. There the physician instructed me in a course of exercises by which a forward curvature of the spine, caused by debility and use of supporters, was remedied, and the figure restored to the natural position, while at the same time the chest, and thus the breathing capacity, were enlarged so as to demand three inches added to waists and belts. Other cases I often have met of similar restoration of the figure, and enlargement of the chest, and compressed lungs, in several health establishments.

In addition to all these, I have tried Sulphur and Vapor baths, Russian baths, Chemical baths, Turkish hot air bath, and the Sun bath, and have seen patients benefited in all. Owing chiefly to my own knowledge and caution I was not injured myself by any, though I saw others, who, from ignorance, imprudence, or want of skill and care in the physician were seriously injured in every one.

I have also met persons who were benefited by the Grape Cure, and the Lifting Cure. Several friends have been treated by an ignorant tailor who taught his patients that the centre of the nervous system was the navel, and that he cured by operations that disentangled the nerves that were gathered in bunches and knots. His method was to spend an hour daily with each patient in a continuous pressure and pinching of all parts of the body, which resulted in some remarkable cures in spite of his ridiculous theories.

My final and only successful experiment was at the Swedish Movement Cure, under the care of Dr. Geo. H. Taylor. This method so far as I have observed, is the most reliable and efficacious remedy for debilitated nerves, and for the internal displacements and diseases consequent on the courses by which so many women weaken the constitution or ruin the health. By this method the weak limb was first relieved, and after this, by a strict obedience to all the laws of health, for several years I have enjoyed perfect health. I have also been every year gaining in strength and in the increased power of faculties usually diminished by age. And should burnings, and crushings of railroads, and other casualties be escaped, I have a fair chance for at least another twenty years of health, and active usefulness.

But this result has been gained not by any one method of medical treatment, but rather by faithful obedience to the laws of health, while it is preserved and continued only by the same. For whenever I failed in any one respect, my enfeebled nervous system, especially the weaker member, reported the wrong with marvelous precision.

What has been gained is continued only by a faithful and diligent course, securing pure air by night and day; regular and abundant sleep in the hours of darkness, and no mental or physical labor except by day; a daily towel bath in cool water in the sun or by a fire, except in hot weather; living in light and well ventilated rooms, and often sitting in the sun; abstinence from stimulating drinks of all kinds; a simple diet of properly cooked food in a moderate quantity, and only at regular hours; daily outdoor exercise by walking, riding, and use of the muscles of the arms and trunk; clothing that never compresses any part and always protects from chills; abstinence from over excitement of all kinds; the cultivation of a cheerful and quiet spirit; healthful amusements; benevolent activity never to exceed the strength; and all this prayerfully pursued as a religious duty owed to God, to my fellow men, and to myself.

Another lesson illustrated by my experience, is the advance of medical science in detecting the *causes* of diseases so as to apply remedies intelligently. My case was simply prostration of the nervous system by mental care and labor, increased by a punctured nerve. And yet my medical advisers, most of them distinguished in their profession, treated me, one, for diseased stomach, another for diseased spine, another for diseased blood, and most of them applied stimulants to the weak part, always thus increasing the weakness. That was nearly forty years ago. Since then nervous diseases are better understood, while animal chemistry, the microscope, and the thermometer have furnished new means for intelligent search for *causes* of disease.

And yet our most learned physicians complain of the deficient education given to medical students, and their negligent practice in comparison with European methods. I have before me the Richmond and Louisville Medical Journal of 1869, which claims to be the largest medical monthly in this nation. In it I find a letter from Dr. W. O. Baldwin, late President of the National Congress of physicians, asking from Dr. Wm. Neftel, of New York, late physician of the Russian Imperial Guard, an account of the course of medical study in Europe, and remarking that Dr. Neftel "beautifully illustrates by his example and by his valuable contributions to science, the wisdom of the system in which he was educated."

In reply, Dr. Neftel states that the first requisition in Europe for medical license, is a course of general study equal to that demanded in our colleges, and in addition, a thorough knowledge of physics. Next follows four summer and four winter sessions in the medical department. The first two years are devoted to anatomy, histology, physiology, chemistry, pathological anatomy, general and special pathology and therapeutics, the principles of operative surgery and obstetrics, working at the same time in the chemical, physiological and pathological laboratories. In the last sessions only the student attends the different clinics—medical, surgical, obstetrical, opthalmological, dermatological, and psychological. Then, under a professor some special branch of medical science is pursued.

Dr. Neftel states as one cause of the advance of medical science in Germany and Russia, is the institution of free teachers or *privat docents*. These are students distinguished by original genius or great research, who in connexion with the faculty, become teachers, and have full access to laboratories, museums, and libraries. Many young physicians of talents thus rise to high positions, and from this class have risen the greatest men of science. Thus it is, also, that the German Universities secure the best professors who devote their lives to science and instruction, with most admirable results.

Another advantage to medical science in Germany, is the close connexion of the medical departments in the Universities with the other faculties of philosophy, law, and theology. In consequence of this, we find the greatest chemists and natural philosophers to be medical men, and a number of physiologists are great mathematicians.

Dr. Neftel, after completing this course, was connected with medical departments in the Universities of London, Paris, and Germany for four years. After this the adoption of republican opinions prevented his return to Russia, and led him to this country.

It is by frequent intercourse with Dr. Neftel, and by observing his methods of detecting the *causes* of disease, that I have been deeply impressed with the imperfect modes pursued by inexperienced practitioners, and even by some who stand high in the profession. For example, I took a friend to him who had been examined by several physicians of high standing. One of them decided that the disease was of the heart, another that it was of the liver, and a third that it was of the kidneys. But by the microscope and by chemical tests, it was proved that neither of these organs were diseased, and that all the symptoms were caused by miasmatic fungi in the blood.

In the case of another lady I witnessed investigations to detect the *cause* of the frequent re-appearance of carbuncles, which had not been sought for by other medical advisers; they only prescribing modes of hastening and diminishing the crisis. To look at the tongue, feel the pulse, and hear a statement of the symptoms, is the common method, and then prescriptions are given of powerful chemical agents, which, if not suited to the case are injurious.

Thus it comes to pass that the most learned and careful physicians are demanding an increase of medical educational advantages in our country.

Thus also it has come to pass that health establishments abound, in which the natural agencies of water, light, pure air, exercise, and simple diet are the chief medical agents employed. And in most cases the patients are those who have vainly tried the regular medical treatment.

The great defect in all these institutions, so far as I have observed, is confinement to one special method, and a neglect of enforcing obedience to *all* the laws of health. For in not even one such institution have I ever known proper arrangements for securing pure air both night and day; while in some the diet is at war with healthful digestion. To these evils add the ignorance of the patients in over-doing, and the want of skill, or care of the physician, and the result has been more mischief than benefit in many cases. For there is as much need of science and care in the physician in the use of these natural agents as in the more common methods.

Recently some of the most efficacious methods employed in Water Cure Establishments have received the sanction and approval of the highest medical practitioners in Europe.

For in the *Medical Record,* the leading periodical of N. York physicians, I find a paper read before the New York Academy of Medicine, in October, 1868, by Dr. Neftel, in which he states that the most distinguished writers and practitioners in Europe now employ cold water for reducing fevers, just as for twenty years or more has been practiced in Water Cures.

In this paper he says: "My first acquaintance with the use of water in diseases, was during the Crimean war, when a murderous epidemic of typhus fever prevailed, *resisting every known method of treatment*. Following the instincts of patients and watching the effects of cold water, I commenced treating with cold sponging and effusions and the result surpassed my hopes, and was *far better than that obtained by any other method*. I myself was attacked by the disease and was saved from death only by my own mode of treatment. But still my treatment was purely empyrical and symptomatic. Soon after, this method was confirmed in the large hospitals of Russia, with excellent results."

"The principal rule observed is never to allow the temperature (ascertained by a thermometer placed under the shoulder) to rise higher than 103 Fahrenheit. The mildest degree of cooling is attained by sponging the whole body with cold water or by keeping the patient continually in a wet sheet. A wet cloth is laid on the head, and if not asleep, every quarter of an hour the patient is offered a little cold water to drink, and every three hours nourishing fluid food. The room is to be kept well ventilated and stimulants avoided."

Dr. Neftel adds, "the effect of this treatment is so wonderful that those familiar with typhoid patients will not recognize them. By keeping the temperature below 103.1 Fahrenheit the exacerbations are avoided and the fever kept in a continuous remission. The patients are never unconscious, never delirious, the tongue always remains moist and clean, the bronchial catarrh is very slight, and so is the diarrhœa, if any at all. There is no tympanites, no hemorrhage, no complication, and we have reason to believe the intestinal ulcerations do not occur at all. Under this treatment the course of typhoid fever is very mild and short, the convalescence very rapid, and the mortality none whatever. A great number of patients treated by myself on this method, have recovered without exception. In this city I had a patient whose morning temperature once reached 106.34° Fahrenheit—*a case absolutely fatal under every other treatment*—and she is now recovering."

"The thermometer indicates with the greatest exactness, the condition of the animal heat, the presence of fever, its degree, intensity and danger. It also traces the laws of the course of different types of disease, indicates transitions from one stage to another, the ameliorations and aggravations, and the return of the normal condition. It enables us to form a correct diagnosis and prognosis, and gives us positive therapeutical indications." In conversation I enquired if all kinds of fevers should be subdued by this method, and was assured that this was the safest and surest mode for all.

A scientific and very successful practitioner who managed a Water Cure Establishment, and was largely employed in the town around, stated that after a year or two of instruction in the use of cold water, he lost all his outside patients, as the mothers and housekeepers had learned to treat by his methods, and no longer needed his attention except in rare cases.

I have stated that it was at the Swedish Movement Cure, under charge of Dr. Geo. H. Taylor, that the cause of my long invalidism and its remedy were ascertained. In addition to this personal benefit, I have learned the cause and the proper remedy of a class of female diseases which have baffled the most skillful practitioners and introduced methods in many ways so unfortunate, that my whole sex will eventually recognize as a great benefactor, the physician who has rendered them needless, and introduced others at once philosophical, modest, and efficacious.

Dr. Taylor's discoveries and methods are presented in his work on the Diseases of Women, published by George Maclean, 47 John Street, N. Y. This work has the approval of the leading physicians of Philadelphia and New York, and other distinguished practitioners whose specialty has been in this department. If this work should find its way into every school and family, it probably would do more for the health of women and of the next generation than any other similar measure that can be urged.

The information I have gained in the modes narrated, has increased my conviction of the importance of giving to every woman a *scientific* training for her profession as *healthkeeper* of the family state. Not that the long course needed for general medical practice should be attempted, which in the chief European Universities would demand ten and twelve years of study and training. Instead of this, I would propose a moderate course in physiology and animal chemistry, accompanied with instruction in practical scientific methods of employing water, light, heat, cold, air, exercise, and diet—both to prevent and to remedy diseases—nor should the application of these remedies be left entirely to the judgment and skill of women, even after such training, but be under the guidance of a physician, highly educated, so as to detect by careful investigation the *causes* of disease, and of such another as Dr. Taylor, who has practised in both the Water and Movement Cures.

I have stated that in one large town a Water Cure physician lost all his outside practice by instructing mothers and housekeepers how to use properly the methods of the Water Cure. If to these were added the practical methods of the Movement Cure, as conducted by Dr. G. H. Taylor, with the enforcement of *all* the laws of health in a given community, it is probable that all the physicians but those superintending these methods, would lose all their practice.

One of the most judicious and well educated physicians I know, expressed the opinion that if a number of families in a town would unite to provide a salary to a good physician (the same as to a clergyman) who should visit each family to watch over the habits and health, and see all methods employed to keep them well, that in the end, it would prove a great piece of economy in money as well as in health. The sagacious Chinese have learned this, and pay their physicians so long as they are well, and stop paying when they are ill.

But with us it is for the pecuniary interest of physicians to have sickness general in a community, and there is need of a profession whose honor and emolument depend on the *prevention* of all diseases. For this profession every woman, and especially every school-teacher should be carefully trained.

If all the women teachers of this nation could be trained to be *health-keepers* under the supervision of the highest class of educated physicians, and then sent forth to lecture in all our school districts teaching mothers and housekeepers the laws of health, and the methods of the Water and Movement Cures, it is probable that health and long life would be doubled all over the nation.

And here I would urge renewed attention to the state of female health in our country as exhibited in statistics published in a work of mine fifteen years ago, and introduced in a chapter placed at the end of this volume. I have never found any reason to doubt the correctness of the impression made by these statements at first, nor to suppose any marked improvement at the present time. For the diminution of domestic labor by school girls of all ages and classes; the increase of mental labor in public schools; the increase of cares to mother and housekeepers in country as well as cities, from increase of the refinements of civilization; the increased use of stoves and furnaces without proper arrangements for ventilation; the increase of unhealthful labor for women in unventilated stores, shops, and mills; the unhealthful fashions of dress, and the fact that at this day women receive more delicate constitutions than those given by mothers of a former generation; all these things indicate an increase rather than a diminution of the causes that undermine the health of women.

This brings me to the main object of this meeting, which is to enlist the interest and influence of the ladies present, in devising and executing plans for the proper education of the daughters of this city—by methods that shall remedy the evils that have been set forth, and which shall serve as a model to other cities and towns through our nation.

In detailing an outline of the plan aimed at, I will first state that it has already received the approval of ladies of good judgment, and of practical experience as mothers and housekeepers; and also is approved by the Trustees of the H. F. Seminary.

I appear at this time as the Secretary and Gen. Agent of the American Woman's Educational Association. This consists of ladies of high character and position in various states which meets annually to receive reports of agents and direct their operations. This Association has established several institutions at the West, the most important being the Milwaukee Female College. The method employed was to take a school already organized as the nucleus, and then offer to the citizens to secure endowments to support teachers, on condition that they provided a suitable building and tuition fees to support a certain number of superior teachers. This was done, and for fifteen years that institution, in its primary, preparatory, and collegiate schools has successfully carried out one portion of the plan of the Association, some teachers being supported by endowments provided by the Association, and others by tuition fees. The chief agent of the Association has had the control and supervision of this institution now numbering nearly 200 pupils from all the Protestant denominations. The chief difficulty has been the fact that the Association is located at the East, and its work done at the West.

It is now proposed to carry out the plans of the Association more completely in an institution at the East, under the immediate charge of an Executive Committee, resident in the same place as the Institution.

It is proposed to organize the H. F. Seminary like that at Milwaukee, with Primary, Preparatory, and Collegiate schools all under the care of the Trustees as at present. These schools to be furnished by the citizens, with building, library, and apparatus equal to those of the High School, and a course of study instituted allowing entrance only at certain periods, and limiting the number of studies each term, as is done in the College and High School. Also to raise endowments to support two of the highest class of teachers, so that they can secure homes and salaries equal to those given to college professors.

This being secured by the citizens, the Association will appoint their Executive Committee from ladies of this city, one from each denomination, and others be added, selected by them, also a certain number of the Trustees of the Seminary to become members. Then the managers will appoint a collecting agent to raise funds to establish a University School with diverse departments, in which pupils of the Seminary and others shall be trained for all the distinctive duties of women, and all who wish it also be trained for some suitable womanly employment or profession by which to earn an honorable independence.

The first organized departments of the University would be the Normal and

Health departments. Two highly educated ladies would become the Principals, and Dr. Neftel, and Dr. Taylor have engaged to act as superintending physicians. The Association will aim to provide land and buildings for these departments, and support the two lady principals so that they can receive into their families two classes. During the months of July and August, when most teachers have vacations, the class will consist of enfeebled and exhausted teachers to be restored and trained to teach our system of Calisthenics, and to administer the methods of the Water Cure, and Movement Cure, and also to lecture on the laws of health in the communities to which they will return.

At all other periods of the year, these families will consist of young girls of delicate constitutions or poor health, to be trained to health and vigor, and at the same time to pursue a moderate course of study in the Seminary classes. These lady principals will also take charge of the Seminary classes in Domestic Science, Physiology, Animal Chemistry, Botany, and Calisthenics under direction of the Principals of the Seminary. On this plan two teachers will be supported by endowments provided by the citizens, and two by endowments provided by the Association.

The Trustees of the Seminary will control all funds given for the Primary, Preparatory, and Collegiate schools, and the Executive Committee of the Association will control the funds given for the University department. As to the probability of raising endowments, the former agent of the Association testifies that he was cordially welcomed to the pulpits of almost every Protestant denomination and sometimes took larger collections than were given for any other objects.

There is one reason for endowing the H. F. Seminary, little understood. Three female institutions are soon to go into operation in Massachusetts, one endowed with a million and a half, another with half a million, a third very largely provided. These will offer advantages and salaries commanding the best teachers, and the public High Schools will do the same. Thus the boarding and other pay schools not endowed, will soon lose their best teachers and take up only with a humbler class. This, and the multiplication of studies and classes, will make boarding and day schools for the wealthy class, unless endowed, very inferior to the public High schools and endowed institutions.

Many female colleges have attempted a regular course of study demanding few classes for each term, and that all pupils enter at regular periods. But not one that I know of, has raised endowments to support teachers. Not even Vassar, though provided with over half a million, has a single endowment to support a teacher. All has been spent in expensive grounds, buildings, and furniture to draw pupils from parental watch and care.

If this half million had been devoted to providing endowments for this Seminary, some ten or twelve of the highest class of women teachers might have permanent positions and incomes.

In reference to the patronage to be expected for the health department, Dr. Dio Lewis gained very large patronage by taking charge of young girls in delicate health who thronged from every part of the nation.

I will close by giving a specimen of the applications constantly made to me from all quarters for teachers out of health. I think if it were notified in the public prints that help could be given to such applications, they would count more by thousands than by hundreds.

So much and so often have I been pained to turn away from such piteous appeals, that nothing but the hope of some day meeting such a sympathizing and influential body of friends and followers of Christ, has sustained me.

> "Dear Miss Beecher:
>
> "Having read of your plans for aiding teachers in regaining health, I address you in behalf of a dear and only child. I myself was a teacher, and by intense interest and labor lost my health. My marriage afterwards was unfortunate, and ever since the birth of this child I have had to struggle alone and with poor health to support her and myself by my needle.
>
> "My child is fond of study, is a graduate of one of the best public schools, and afterward attended an excellent Grammar school in N. York city. The principal told me she was the brightest in her class, and had a depth and clearness of mind unusual in her age. She was much beloved in her classes, especially by her teachers.
>
> "But her studies were too severe, and for a long time she has not been able to study or do much except practice on the piano, for which she had the best of teachers, and would like to teach it when her head gets stronger. I have consulted one of the best physicians, and he says she may recover in time, that too much study is the cause of her trouble, and that she must not study at all.
>
> "Dear Miss Beecher, you cannot imagine how great is my interest in your plans, and how I long to place my daughter under your care. I thought the anxieties of a mother would prove some claim on your kindness, and that you would excuse me for applying to you for advice and help. If my child could go into some christian home near the sea-side and do light work to pay for her board, she would be willing to do so; and perhaps could teach one or two scholars in music. The poor child now feels distressed and discouraged, and I know not what to do. She is a Christian believer and a member of the church, and I hope our Heavenly Father will show us some way of help and comfort in this our low estate."

An Address to the Christian Women of America.

My Dear and Honored Countrywomen:

When I wrote the first address in this volume, I had a very imperfect idea of the scope and magnitude of the questions which the women of this nation, who aim to be followers of Jesus Christ, will soon be called to investigate and to decide—questions which are the very foundation principles of both morals and religion—questions which every woman must settle for herself aided by common sense, the Bible, and the Divine aid obtained by prayer.

To us Jesus Christ appears as the only one born into this world who lived to maturity, then died and then returned to life again; first to prove that death does not end our existence, and next to teach what awaits us in the invisible world to which we all are hastening.

Let those who have mused in lonely sorrow by the grave of the dearest friends and asked with infinite longings—where are they? is this the end? are we too to lie down in utter annihilation?—say how we could have these questions answered so as to best secure a comforting belief? Should we not say let our well-known, well-beloved friends, come forth from the tomb and live with us again—walk, talk, eat, sleep, and act, as in past times—and this for days and weeks and not alone with us, but with many others who had known them through life? Can we imagine anything to ask more satisfactory than this, to prove that death does not end our existence?

Suppose that Abraham Lincoln, after his body had lain in state for three days, had risen from his coffin and for thirty days had been surrounded by his family, his cabinet, his personal friends, and by as many as three hundred persons who knew him well; can we conceive of anything more satisfactory to prove that death does not destroy the soul? And would not his honest teachings of what is to be experienced after death, be sought as the most reliable evidence possible of what awaits us all when we pass to the invisible world?

This is exactly what the believers in the Christian religion claim was done for us when Jesus Christ came and dwelt on earth for thirty-three years, then was slain by enemies determined to prevent his predicted resurrection, and then arose from the dead, bringing life and immortality to light. And why did this good Being come and dwell on earth, then die, and then arise from the dead? It was to teach us not only that an immortal existence stretches before us after death, but that the happiness of that immortality depends on *the character which is formed by education here.*

What then is the character which we are to seek in order to attain immortal blessedness? The first sermon of our Lord has this very topic as its burden:

"Blessed are the poor in spirit,"—those who feel the need of knowledge, guidance, and help.

"Blessed are the meek,"—those that receive rebuke and instruction without anger.

"Blessed are they that do hunger and thirst after righteousness,"—those that long to know what is the right way, and to walk in it.

"Blessed are the *happiness makers,*"[3]—those who make happiness the right way, as taught by the Master—"for they are the children of God,"—having His nature as the child has the father's nature, and they are to dwell with Him forever.

It is such who are to "rejoice and be exceeding glad" even when persecuted, hated, and reviled, for right words and actions. It is such who are to enter the kingdom of Heaven.

And what is this kingdom? It is one made up of the righteous, those who long to know what is right and to do it, who hunger and thirst after righteousness, and so are forever to be satisfied. And then the Master teaches that His kingdom is not of this world, but exactly the opposite. For the children of this world do not feel poor in spirit, but rather seek to be called Rabbi, and to teach others. They do not wish to be told of their ignorance, mistakes and sins, and are angry when it is done. They do not hunger and thirst to find the lowly way of righteousness, but rather the way of riches, honor, and power.

They do not seek to become true "happiness makers" as taught by the words and example of the Master, taking a humble place, going about and doing good, and working for others more than for self. Instead of this they work and plan for self, first, and then for those belonging to self, and care little for the world that the Master came to save. They seek to be at the top and to have all below look up to them.

Now the family state is instituted to educate our race to the Christian character,—to train the young to be followers of Christ. Woman is its chief minister, and the work to be done is the most difficult of all, requiring not only intellectual power but a moral training nowhere else so attainable as in the humble, laborious,

[3] This is a more exact translation than "Blessed are the peace-makers."

daily duties of the family state.

Woman's great mission is to train immature, weak, and ignorant creatures, to obey the laws of God; the physical, the intellectual, the social, and the moral—first in the family, then in the school, then in the neighborhood, then in the nation, then in the world—that great family of God whom the Master came to teach and to save. And His most comprehensive rule is, "Thou shall love the Lord thy God with all thy heart," and "this is the love of God that ye keep His commandments." And next, "Thou shalt love thy neighbor as thyself." These two the Master teaches are the chief end of man and includes all taught by Moses and the prophets. This then is woman's work, to train the young in the family and the school *to obey God's laws* as learned partly by experience, partly by human teaching and example, and partly by revelations from God.

But the most solemn duty of the Christian woman is the *motives* she is to employ in training to this obedience. The motives used by the worldly educator are the gain or loss of earthly pleasures, honors, and comforts. But the truly Christian woman feels and presents as the grand motive, the dangers of the future life from which our Lord came to save us, and these so dreadful that all we most value in this life are to be made secondary and subordinate, while the chief concern is, not mainly to save self, but rather to save ourselves by laboring to save others from ignorance of God's laws and to secure the obedience indispensable to future eternal safety.

And this is to be done at a period when this great motive of Christ's religion is more and more passing out of regard, even in the Christian church. So much is this the case, that the world has good reason to say that while most creeds and preachers teach it in words, few really believe it. For "it is actions that speak louder than words," as to what is believed.

For example, if a company of amiable persons were told that a shipwreck was close at hand and help needed to save the struggling passengers, and yet, after a few enquiries, all went on as before, it would justly be said that these persons do not believe in the messenger and his message. But suppose another company, on hearing the news, rush out amid the darkness and danger, to help; this would prove their *faith* in the messenger and his story.

Now no earthly danger can compare with those revealed by our Lord as threatening every child born into this life; and He also teaches that *the number saved depends on the self-denying labors of His followers*. With small exceptions, all the Christian churches profess to believe this, and that the first concern of Christian life is to *save as many as possible*. And yet where is the *practical* evidence that this is believed?

If these teachings of Christ were fully and practically believed, would it not so divide the church from the world that there could be no mistake as to who are Christians and who are not? And is there any such marked divisions in most of our churches?

It may be urged that this doctrine has been set forth with such hideous detail and additions entirely unwarranted by the Bible and so abhorrent to the best feelings of humanity, that the more men become humane and Christ-like the more they revolt from it.[4]

Yet if this be so, the fact remains that Jesus Christ, the only reliable messenger from the invisible world, has in the strongest language both literal and figurative, set forth these dangers and enjoined on his followers as their *first* concern, to save as many as possible, by training them to a knowledge of God's laws and to habitual obedience to them. And is there not a want of *belief* in this—that is, a want that *practical faith* in Christ and his message, which it is the great and chief mission of woman to secure by her ministry in the family and school? She it is who daily is to train all under her care to become *righteous,* that is, to *feel and act right* according to the rules of right revealed by Jesus Christ. She is to teach that "repentance" which consists in such sorrow for wrong doing as involves turning from it, and such love as secures obedience to the Lord and Savior.

Now the Christian woman in the family and in the school is the most complete autocrat that is known, as the care of the helpless little ones, the guidance of their intellect, and the formation of all their habits, are given to her supreme control. Scarcely less is she mistress and autocrat over a husband, whose character, comfort, peace, and prosperity, are all in her power. In this responsible position is she to teach, by word and example, as did Jesus Christ? Is she to set an example to children and servants not only of that of a ruler, but also of obedience as a subordinate? In the civil state her sons will be subjects to rulers who are weak and wicked, just as she may be subject to a husband and father every way her inferior in ability and moral worth. Shall she teach her children and servants by her own example to be humble, obedient, meek, patient, forgiving, gentle, and loving, even to the evil and unthankful, or shall she form rebellious parties and carry her points by contest and discord? God has given man the physical power, the power of the purse, and the civil power, and woman must submit with Christian equanimity or contend. What is the answer of common sense, and what are the teachings of Christ and His Apostles?

Let every woman who is musing on these questions, take a reference Bible and examine all the New Testament directions on the duties of the family state, and she will have no difficulty in deciding what was the view of Christ and His Apostles as to woman's position and duties. She is a *subordinate* in the family state, just as her father, husband, brother, and sons are subordinates in the civil state. And the same rules that are to guide them are to guide her. She and they are to be obedient to "the higher powers"—those that can force obedience—except when their demands are contrary to the higher law of God, and in such a conflict they are "to obey God rather than man," and take the consequences whatever they may be. And a woman has no more difficulty in deciding when to obey God rather than man in the family state than her husband, father, and sons have, in the civil state. And obedience in the family to "the higher power" held by man, is no more

[4] Note C.

a humiliation than is man's obedience to a civil ruler.

If this be so, then the doctrine of woman's subjugation is established and the opposing doctrine of Stuart Mills and his followers is in direct opposition to the teachings both of common sense and Christianity.

There is a moral power given to woman in the family state much more controlling and abiding than the inferior, physical power conferred on man. And the more men are trained to refinement, honor, and benevolence, the more this moral power of woman is increased. This is painfully illustrated in cases where an amiable and Christian man is bound for life to an unreasonable, selfish, and obstinate woman. With such a woman reasoning is useless, and physical force alone can conquer, and this such a man cannot employ. The only alternatives are ceaseless conflicts, at the sacrifice of conscience and self-respect, or hopeless submission to a daily and grinding tyranny.

The general principles to guide both men and women as to the duties of those in a subordinate station, have been made clear by discussions relating to civil government. But the corresponding duties of those invested with power and authority have not been so clearly set forth, especially those of the family state. While the duties of subordination, subjection, and obedience, have been abundantly enforced on woman, the corresponding duties of man as head and ruler of the family state have not received equal attention either from the pulpit or the press. And this is not because they are not as difficult, as important and as clearly taught by the Master and the Apostles of Christianity.

St. Paul, who, while he dwelt in retirement in Arabia, received the direct instructions of Jesus Christ, claims to have full authority from the Master to instruct on this important and fundamental topic, and in his Epistle to the Ephesians we have his express and full teachings. In this most interesting passage we find that the family state is the emblem to represent Jesus Christ and the Church—the Church "which is the great company of faithful people" in all ages and all lands—those who are appointed to guide and save the world—the true educators of our race, who, by self-denying labors are to train men for Heaven. Of this body the Apostles teaches that Jesus Christ is the head—those whom He has redeemed by His labor and sacrifice, and who are to train as His children all whom they can rescue from ignorance and sin, by similar labor and sacrifice.

It is in this connection that he sets forth the duties of the family state, Ephesians v: 22 to 33, "Wives submit yourselves unto your own husbands *as unto the Lord*. For the husband is head of the wife, even as Christ is head of the Church: Therefore, as the Church is subject to Christ so let the wives be to their own husbands in everything."

"Husbands love your wives even as Christ also loved the Church and gave Himself for it, that He might sanctify and cleanse it with the washing of water by the word, that He might present it to Himself, a glorious Church, not having spot or wrinkle or any such thing, but that it should be holy and without blemish. So ought men to love their wives as their own bodies. He that loveth his wife loveth himself. For no man ever yet hated his own flesh, but nourisheth and cherisheth it even as the Lord the Church. For we are members of His body, of His flesh, and of His bones. For this cause shall a man leave his father and mother and shall be joined unto his wife, and they two shall be one flesh."

No wonder these directions close with "this is a great mystery"; for the most advanced followers of Christ have but just begun to understand the solemn relations and duties of the family state—man the head, protector, and provider—woman the chief educator of immortal minds—man to labor and suffer to train and elevate woman for her high calling, woman to set an example of meekness, gentleness, obedience, and self-denying love, as she guides her children and servants heavenward.

It is this comprehensive view of the family state as organized to train immortal minds for the eternal world that indicates the reason for the stringency of the teachings of our Lord as to the indissoluble union of man and wife in marriage.

> "And he said unto them, Moses, *because of the hardness of your hearts*, suffered you to put away your wives; but from the beginning it was not so. And I say unto you, whosoever shall put away his wife, except it be for fornication, and shall marry another committeth adultery; and whosoever marrieth her that is put away doth commit adultery."
>
> "Have ye not read that He which made them at the beginning made them male and female, and said, For this cause shall a man leave father and mother and shall cleave to his wife, and they twain shall be one flesh. What therefore God hath joined together let not man put asunder."

This then is "the higher law" which abrogates all contrary human statutes and forbids to marry more than once, except when death or adultery breaks the bond. This statute brings all the advocates of free divorce in direct antagonism with the teachings of Jesus Christ. And it is a striking fact that the great body of those who advocate free divorce and free love, deny the authority of Jesus Christ as the authorized teacher of faith and morals.

In the discussions as to woman's rights and wrongs, it is assumed on one side that she is not to take a subordinate position either in the family or the State. And the apparent plausibility of the claim is owing to a want of logical clearness in the use of words. When it is said that "all men are created free and equal and equally entitled to life, liberty, and the pursuit of happiness," and that women as much as men are included, it is true in one use of terms and false in another. It is true in this sense, that woman's happiness and usefulness are equal in value to man's, and ought to be so treated. But it is not true that women are and should be treated as the equals of men in *every* respect. They certainly are not his equals in physical power, which is the final resort in *government* of both the family and the State. And it is owing to this fact that she is placed as a subordinate both in the family and the State. At the same time it is required of man who is holding "the higher powers" so to administer that woman shall have equal advantages with man for usefulness and happiness.

Hitherto the laws relating to women in the civil state have been formed on the assumption that society is a combination of families, in each of which the husband and father is the representative head, and the one who, it is supposed, will secure all that is just and proper for the protection and well being of wife and daughters. And if the teachings of Christianity were dominant, and every man loved his wife as himself, and was ready to sacrifice himself and suffer for her elevation and improvement, even as Christ suffered to redeem and purify the Church, there would be no trouble.

But both men and women have been selfish and sinful, neither party having attained the high ideal of Christianity, and very many have not even understood it so as to aim at it. But it is woman's mission as the educator of the race to remedy the evil, not by giving up the ideal but by striving more and more to conform herself and all under her care to its blessed outlines. And in past times those families have been the most peaceful and prosperous where the wife and mother has most faithfully aimed to obey the teachings of Christ and His Apostles, in this as in every other direction.

The principle of subordination is the great bond of union and harmony through the universe. At the head is the loving Father and Lord whom all are to obey with perfect faith and submission. Then revelations teaches that in the invisible world are superior and subordinate ranks, each owing obedience to superiors in station and described as "thrones, dominions, principalities, and powers." Again, in this world are also superiors and subordinates, not only in the family state but in all kinds of business where heads of establishments and master workmen demand implicit faith and obedience.

This being so, one of the most important responsibilities of a woman in the family state is to train the young in this duty, not only by precept but also by example. And a woman who clearly understands the importance of this, will pride herself on her implicit obedience to the official head of the family state, as much so as the citizen or soldier does to his superior officer, or the subordinate operator to his master-workman.

But at the same time, such a woman will demand and expect a return for this submission, that the husband and father fulfil his corresponding and more difficult duties; to love his wife as himself; to honor her as *physically* the weaker vessel needing more tender care and less exposure and labor; to suffer for her in order to increase her improvement, usefulness, and happiness, even as the Lord suffered to elevate and purify his followers.

The duty of subordination, though so fundamental and important, is one to which all minds are naturally averse. For every mind seeks to follow its own judgment and wishes rather than those of another. Especially is this the case with persons of great sensibilities and strong will. It is owing to this that so many women of this class are followers of Stuart Mills' doctrine that a wife is not a subordinate in the family state. And it is for want of clear instruction on this subject from the pulpit and the press that this doctrine spreads so fast and so widely.

The agitation at the present time in regard to woman's right and wrongs is greatly owing to the fact that, from various causes, large multitudes of women are without the love and protection secured by marriage. And yet the laws and customs of society are framed on the general rule that every man is to be head of a family and every woman a wife. But war, emigration, vicious indulgencies, and many other causes have rendered marriage impossible to multitudes of women; counting by tens of thousands in the older States, and by hundreds of thousands in our nation. A large portion of these women must earn their own independence, while those who are provided with a support are embarrassed by false customs or unjust laws. In regard to the multitudes of women who flock to our cities and to such direful temptations it is often said, why "do they not become servants in families?" Let any woman who has a young daughter ponder this question as one that may reach her own family. Does not almost every woman feel, more or less, the bondage of *caste* and shrink from taking the *lowest place* even though the Lord of Glory set the example?

And is it not the chief attraction toward our pitying Saviour that He loves and tenderly cares for the weak, the wandering and the lost? And are we not walking in His steps when we try to help the weak and foolish who will not take care of themselves?

That there is an emergency which demands changes in our customs and laws, all well informed and benevolent persons will concede. But the main question is, what should be the nature of these changes and how shall they be secured?

There are certain customs of society which are based on the assumption that all women are to marry and be supported by husbands, and that all men are to provide for the support of a family. It is on this assumption that, in cases where men and women do the same work and do it equally well, men receive much larger wages than women.

But as emigration, war, and the vices of unrestrained civilization have interfered with this normal condition of society, the laws and customs should be modified to meet the emergency. For there are many wrongs, both to married and unmarried women, consequent on the present false and unchristian state of things.

As one example of injustice, it is granted by all who superintend public schools, that women are as good and often better teachers than men, and yet they are unjustly denied equal compensation. In many other directions the same unjust custom prevails. Still more unjust is the custom which gives superior advantages to men for the scientific and practical training for a profession by which an honorable independence may be secured and almost none at all are provided for women.

So also in the distribution of public offices of trust and emolument which secure an income from the civil state, there are several in which woman can perform the duties as well or better then men, especially in the care of schools, hospitals, jails, and all public institutions of benevolence.

Almost all persons of intelligence will concede that justice and mercy call for changes and improvement in these particulars. The main question is, what is the best method for securing such improvement?

The party of men and women who are demanding woman suffrage claim that this is the only sure and effective remedy for these and all other wrongs that oppress women both in the family and in the civil state. The party is organized and led by intelligent, energetic, and benevolent women; they have well-conducted periodicals to urge their views and to excite sympathy by details of the various ways in which women suffer from unjust customs and laws; and they are sustained by the approval and co-operation of many gentlemen of talents and benevolence.

But the great majority of intelligent and benevolent men and women are opposed to this measure, first, on account of the probable evils involved and next because the good aimed at may be secured by a safer, more speedy, and more appropriate method.

In enumerating the evils that would result from introducing woman to the responsibilities and excitements of political life, the most prominent is her increased withdrawal from the more humble, but more important offices of the family state. At the present time, the services of the seamstress and the mantua-maker are imperfectly supplied, and when obtained it is often from those who are poorly trained. An economical, trustworthy, and competent cook, is a treasure growing more and more rare, which often the highest wages cannot procure. A kind, intelligent, and affectionate woman, to aid a mother in the cares of the nursery, is still more rare.

If the good mothers and grandmothers, who have trained their own offspring, would take pity on the young mothers all over the land who are suffering for want of just such sympathy and help as only such women can bestow, they would soon find, especially in the poorer classes, a field of usefulness far more in keeping with the tender spirit of Christian love and humility than any offices that political action would provide.

Again, the demand for well trained governesses and family teachers is unsupplied, while multitudes of children all over the nation have no teachers and no schools of any kind. To open avenues to political place and power for all classes of women would cause these humble labors of the family and school to be still more undervalued and shunned.

Another evil to be apprehended from introducing women into political life is increasing the temptations to draw them from the humble, self-sacrificing Christian labor among the ignorant and neglected, which now is so imperfectly supplied. To be a member of the Legislature, a member of Congress, a Judge, a Governor, or a President, are temptations heretofore unknown to women. Who shall say what would be the result should every woman of *every class in society* be stimulated by such temptations?

Another danger to be feared, is the introducing into political strifes the distinctive power of sex, an element as yet untried in our form of government. In some short experiments that have been made we have seen how pure and intelligent women can be deceived and misled by the baser sort, their very innocence and inexperience making them credulous and the helpless tools of the guilty and bold.

Another danger from universal woman suffrage would result from the course that would be taken by many of the most virtuous and intelligent women. Of those who would regard this measure as an act of injustice and oppression, forcing duties on their sex unsuited to their character and circumstances, many would refuse to assume any such responsibilities. Thus a large number of the most intelligent and conscientious women would be withdrawn from the polls, increasing the relative proportion of the ignorant and incompetent voters, a class that already bring doubt on the success of republican institutions. On the other hand, another portion would be forced to the polls by conscientious motives, and there meet the lowest and vilest of their sex as those who are to appoint their rulers and decide their laws. How would it be possible for such women to honor the rulers and respect the laws instituted by such agencies?

The final objection to universal woman suffrage is that there is another safer, surer, and more speedy method at command which would secure all the benefits aimed at without any of these dangers.

This method is based on the general principle that in seeking either favors or rights it is a wise policy to assume the good character and good intentions of those who have the power to give or withhold. The law-making power is now in the hands of men, and the advocates of women suffrage practically are saying, "you men are so selfish and unjust that you cannot be trusted with the interests of your wives, daughters, and sisters; therefore give them the law-making power that they may take care of themselves."

As a mere matter of policy, to say nothing of justice, how much wiser it would be to assume that men are ready and willing to change unjust laws and customs whenever the better way is made clear and then to ask to have all evils that laws can remedy removed. Whenever this course has been practiced it has always been successful and therefore should first be tried. For any men who would give up the law-making power to women in order to remedy existing evils, would surely be those most ready to enact the needful laws themselves.

The woman suffrage party is so extensively organized, with such energetic and persistent leaders and such ably conducted papers and tracts, that those of our sex who are opposed to this measure begin to feel disturbed and anxious lest it should finally be consummated. Instead of meeting this danger by ridicule and obloquy I would suggest that practical methods be instituted in which conservative men and women can unite, and which the most radical will approve and aid.

There are many ways in which great influence can be exerted without any regular organization or establishing newspapers or circulating tracts as is now so vigorously carried on by those favoring woman suffrage. One method might be enlisting editors of newspapers and magazines to promote the circulation of this little volume and also to insert extracts of some of the most effective portions in their columns. Another might be to present this work to the clergymen and seek their influence and counsel in promoting its aims.[5]

Still another might be, efforts to promote the establishment of such a University for Women as the one here indicated, commencing with seeking endowments for the Health and Domestic departments in connection with some flourishing literary institution, for the purpose of restoring women teachers to health, and also for training pupils to become health-keepers in families, schools, and communities.

The importance of this last measure will appear in the following extract from a public address of a regularly educated American physician:

> It is much to be deplored that we have no chair devoted to *Hygiene* in any of our medical colleges. During four courses of Lectures, that I attended, one of them in Paris, I never heard a single lecture upon the Laws of Health; and when on one occasion I asked one of our Professors if he would not devote one or more of his course to this subject, he replied, that he ought to, but feared he would not find time; and then jokingly remarked, that we would find it more to our interests to learn how to cure people than to keep them well; that we would get gratitude and money for healing the sick, but neither the one nor the other for preserving the health of the people, however well we might do it.
>
> I have since found that there was more truth in the remark then I was then willing to admit. Still, I cannot help thinking that we should have such Lectures in every medical school, if for no other purpose but to enable its graduates to heal the sick—confident that more can be gained in this way by a thorough knowledge of Hygiene, than by any other means whatever. No drug or medicine is as powerful for good in disease as a wise advantage of Nature's laws.
>
> We spent in one Session over three weeks in the study of Mercury, its different preparations, effects, etc.; not one hour in learning the value of Light, Air, Sleep, Food, and Clothing. The result

[5] A small periodical, published in Baltimore, Md., entitled the True Woman, ably edited by Mrs. Charlotte E. McKay, is valuable as a cheap and excellent tract with the same aim.

> was we know much about Calomel, and literally nothing about the Laws of Health; so we sat, something over four hundred students, for five or six hours daily, in a room—an amphitheatre—the seats extending from the floor to the ceiling—so small, that another hundred could not possibly be packed into it—and not a window opened all winter—no ventilation whatever—a regular "black hole of Calcutta"—the air heavy, foul, offensive with bad breaths—the odors of tobacco, liquor, onions—poisonous in the extreme—not a fresh cheek among the four hundred. Many of the students drank; most of them used tobacco, coffee, sausages, pork, in short lived like barbarians. A large proportion of them were ill all the time, and some died before the session closed, others soon after, and many since. The professors themselves were often ailing—not very healthy men. If any of my readers will step into any of the medical lectures in any of the colleges of this city, some winter afternoon, he will be able to verify the truth of this description. Their presiding genius seems to have no respect for fresh air, sunlight—in short for the laws of health. How then shall these schools inspire respect for these laws in others? How can they teach them when they know so little of them?

Dr. Willard Parker, of New York, in a recent public address also has lamented the fact that a Woman's Medical College should be the first one sustaining a Chair for instructing in Hygiene, as if it were a conceded fact that it is not the business of physicians to *prevent* disease in a community, but only to cure their patients with medicines.

Is it not a proper time and measure for the women of our country to ask for benefactions, both private and legislative, to secure equal advantage for their professional duty as *health-keepers*, such as have so long and so liberally been bestowed on men to train them for their professions?

Believing that such a measure would meet wide approval, the following form of petition is drawn up, which might be used in every State:

> *To the honorable members of the Senate and House of Representatives of the State of — —:*
>
> We the undersigned, ladies of the State of — — and gentlemen citizens of the same, respectfully petition that an appropriation be made to endow one department of a *Woman's University* under charge of the Trustees of — — Seminary; the object of which shall be to train school-teachers and house-keepers in all that relates to health in schools and families, and that this endowment be made equal to what has been or may be given to endow Scientific Schools for young men; and also that this be given on condition that the citizens of the place give an equal sum to promote the scientific and practical training of women for their distinctive pro-

fessions.

It is believed that there is not a single state in the Union where such a petition signed by a large portion of the intelligent women of the state, would fail. The difficulty is not that the fathers, husbands, and brothers are not ready to bestow all that such women would unite in asking, but rather that women do not so feel the importance of such measures as to unite in such a petition.

It appears in the preceding pages that the daughters of the more wealthy classes who are educated in boarding schools and most academies and female colleges cannot enjoy advantages equal to what are given gratuitously in our best public High Schools to the children of the poor. Instead of following in the rear of public schools, those who have wealth should aim to elevate the public schools by the example of institutions of the highest order for their own daughters. And they also would be doubly blest if they would set an example that should both dignify labor and protect their daughters from helpless poverty should reverses come, by having them *trained to some profession* by which they could earn an honorable independence.

When the precepts and example of Jesus Christ fully interpermeate society, to labor with the hands will be regarded not only as a duty but a privilege.

TO THE FORMER PUPILS AND PERSONAL FRIENDS OF THE WRITER.

If this enterprise succeeds in Connecticut its example will be followed in other States, and this volume is sent to many former pupils and personal friends that they may co-operate in the several ways suggested.

As the writer in former times has received such aid and co-operation, with funds also to employ at her discretion, and for several years has had no official organs to report results, it is proper to state that her personal expenditures for many years have been in a style of economy which she has seen practised to such a degree nowhere else, and that *all* her income not thus employed has been devoted to plans from aiding her own sex to prepare for and perform their sacred ministry.

The question as to *how much* of our income it is *our duty* to give for the cause for which our Lord came and suffered is a difficult one to settle. But He instructed the rich young man, "Sell all that thou hast and give to the poor and come and follow us," and he also approved the poor widow who gave her last mite to the service of God.

In following out the spirit of these teachings, even in this life, to the writer has been fulfilled His gracious promise, "Give and it shall be given, good measure, pressed down, shaken together, running over." And the added rewards will increase through eternal ages, as immortal spirits, rescued from ignorance and sin, will carry forward the same noble work of training immortal minds to virtue and happiness.

Those who spend their money and time for earthly enjoyments that perish in the using "have their reward" in the short lived pleasures. Those who most literally follow the Divine Master lay up treasures that fail not, but draw interest through everlasting ages. This is written for the comfort and encouragement of those who by the writer were trained to "seek *first* the kingdom of God and His righteousness."

Notes

Note A.

Note A. Mrs. Livermore, in her address which followed this, expressed the wish that I had noticed more directly the main point, (i. e.) woman's natural, as well as constitutional right to the ballot. This I will briefly attempt here.

It will be conceded by all, that neither man nor woman has any right to anything which is contrary to the *best* good of society. The question then is, does the best good of society demand a *division of responsibilities*, so that man shall take those out of the family, and woman those in it? In other words, shall man take the responsibilities of nursery and kitchen in addition to his outside business, and shall women take charge of government, war, and the work men must do in addition to her home duties? Past laws and customs demand the division, and it is probable that it will be retained.

As to the constitution of the United States, and the 14th and 15th amendments, the question all turns on the use of the terms *citizen* and *people*. Both these words, (as the dictionaries show,) have two uses, a wide, and a limited. In the widest sense they include men, women, and children. In the limited sense they include only a portion of society with certain qualifications which the *best* good of society requires. It is not probable that any court will ever decide that the framers of the constitution, or of the two amendments, used these terms in the widest sense, thus including not only women, but children.

If the best good of society requires women to be law-makers, judges and juries, she has a right to these offices; if it does not, she has no right to them. As to taxation, it is probable that the best good of society *does* require that *women holding property* shall have the ballot, for this would increase the proportion of responsible and intelligent voters, and not add a mass of irresponsible and ignorant ones, as would universal woman suffrage.

It is owing to this that in Europe the statesmen are aiming to give suffrage, not to *all* women as demanded here, but only to those who hold property and pay taxes; for this, in reality, is a method of increasing the proportion of intelligent voters. And if this measure were adopted here it probably would add to the safety of our institutions.

It is worthy of notice that a large portion of those who demand woman suffrage are persons who have not been trained to reason, and are chiefly guided by their generous sensibilities. Such do not seem to be aware that all *reasoning* consists in the presentation of evidence to prove that a given proposition is included in a more general one already believed and granted, and also that in this process there must be definitions of the sense in which terms are used that have several meanings.

Instead of this, they write and talk as if *reasoning* were *any kind* of writing or talking which tends to convince people that some doctrine or measure is true and right. And so they deal abundantly in exciting narratives and rhetorical declamations, and employ words in all manner of deceptive senses.

For example, when Mrs. Livermore pleads that women should have equal rights with men before law, everybody grants it in *some* sense. But the question is in what sense is she to be made equal? All will allow that law should be so framed that woman's highest usefulness and happiness shall be treated as equal in value to that of man's. But this is not relevant to the question whether laws be framed by fathers, husbands, and brothers, or by women. Most women believe that it is for their best good that the responsibility of making and enforcing laws be taken by men and not by women.

But however clearly these distinctions are urged, Mrs. Livermore and her party will keep on saying that women should be made equal with men before the law, without stating in what sense they used these terms. So also they will insist that all "citizens" and all the "people" have a right to vote, without stating what they mean by "a right," or in which sense they use the words "people" and "citizens."

Note B.

Note B. The author of this volume is preparing a new edition of her works on Domestic Science and Economy with many improvements. Its name is to be *The Housekeeper and Healthkeeper*, and it is designed for a complete Encyclopædia of Domestic Science and Practice. It will be published this winter by the Harpers.

It will offer these new and peculiar features:

1. The recipes for food and drink will be in two portions. The first portion will embrace a *very* large collection of simple and economical dishes, which, according to *all* medical and physiological rules, are *perfectly healthful*. The second portion will be a collection of more elaborate and expensive articles, which, according to *all* rules, are of at least doubtful character as to healthfulness. Thus, every housekeeper will have safe and intelligent guidance in her selections.

2. There will be *exact directions* as to *flavors and seasonings*, such as in most re-

ceipt-books are to be "according to the taste," thus leaving young housekeepers to the mercies of untrained cooks.

3. It will contain exact directions for preserving and restoring health by the *scientific* use of the *natural agencies* of water, heat, cold, light, diet, exercise, and pure air, and such only as will be approved by scientific men of *all* medical schools.

Note C.

Note C. All the creeds of the large Christian denominations agree in the following, viz.: that God created angels and our first parents with a "holy nature," and also created such a constitution of things, that by a single sin they changed their holy nature to a "depraved nature" and also transmitted to all their posterity not the holy nature but the depraved one. In consequence of this constitution of things made by God, all our race, except those who are "regenerated," go to everlasting misery in Hell.

As intelligence and Christian feeling have increased, multitudes educated in these views deny the doctrine of future punishments and hold that the righteous and the wicked all go to Heaven at death.

Others hold that God creates all infant minds perfect as to *nature*, being "in his image," yet imperfect in development, and that holy *character* and action can be secured only by training, knowledge and self-control; that "the deeds done in the body" influence character and happiness through an eternal existence; that *some* form such a character in this life as secures eternal happiness and that *some*, by voluntary resistance to the highest possible good influences, form a changeless character of selfishness and consequent misery, so that it were "better never to have been born"; that with others the training to virtue goes on during the intermediate state, in Hades where Christ, at his death, went and preached to those that lived before the flood; (see I Peter, 3: 18, 19, 20,) that the day of judgment is the time when the final separation of the righteous and the wicked will take place; that the punishment of the wicked is only the natural result of perpetuated selfishness in a world from which all the good are removed; and that this separation will not take place until God and all good beings have done all in their power to rescue as many as possible from selfishness and sin.

There are many modifications of these general views in various denominations; but all except a small number agree that Christ teaches that there are awful dangers in the life to come; and that it should be the chief aim of every parent and educator to train all within the reach of their influence so to live and act in view of these dangers as to follow Him in self-denying labors to save as many as possible.

It will be found that in all ages the *fear* of dangers in the life to come has been the basis of the most earnest labor and self sacrifice to save men from ignorance and sin. "The *fear* of the Lord is the *beginning* of wisdom," and those who throw aside this principle loose the most powerful motive in training to safety both for this and the future life. And there are modes of presenting this doctrine so as not to implicate the justice and mercy of our Heavenly Father as do some representations from which humanity more and more revolts.

The fact that sin and suffering exist in a universe created by a perfectly benevolent, wise, and almighty Being, is proof that "almighty power" is not the power to work contradictions, and therefore *in this respect* is limited. In the words of my venerated father, "God cannot govern the stars by the ten commandments, nor free agents by the attraction of gravity." This limitation of God's power in governing free agents, is expressly taught in the Bible. For our only idea of power is causing anything by *willing* it, and *want* of power is inability to cause a thing by willing it. And God repeatedly declares that he is not willing that any should perish; and that he did all for the people of Israel that he could do to make them obedient.

The parents and teachers who hold that *all* are to come out good and happy at last, however negligent or criminal in this life, or that *all* have a second probation, never can train the young to the self-denying labors to save men which Jesus Christ has taught by both precept and example, to be the duty of his followers. It is very certain that the whole course of my life would have been changed for the worse had I believed either that there was little or no danger in the life to come or that *all* had a second probation after death.

Note D.

Note D. The following chapter is a part of my small work entitled *Letters to the People on Health and Happiness,* published by the Harpers, who have loaned the stereotype plates here used.

Before reading it, I would ask that my *definitions* be borne in mind when I class the degrees of health, and also the fact that when I give my own observations I am confined to those persons whom I know well enough to ascertain exactly their state of health, while there may be others in close vicinity not noticed, whom on enquiry I might find to be vigorously healthy women.

Every woman who has any kind of liability to be a mother, or a nurse of the sick, or to meet other exhausting emergencies of the family state needs a *reserved* force of vital strength which many women who seem to be in perfect health find lacking in such emergencies. This want of this is one cause of the frequent failure of health after marriage, and is one result of a transmitted delicate constitution.

I also ask special attention to the fact that women in the country of the industrial classes have not the robust health of earlier generations. In addition to other causes, for this, is the overworking and anxiety consequent on increased civilization. The fashions and expenditures of cities stimulate the country, and the mothers strain every nerve to secure for sons and daughters a style of dress and furniture in former days unknown. This and the desire to accumulate, wears out many a wife and mother before half her days are accomplished, making her a perpetual invalid or sending her to an early grave.

Letter Eighteenth.

Statistics of Female Health.

During my extensive tours in all portions of the Free States, I was brought into most intimate communion, not only with my widely-diffused circle of relatives, but with very many of my former pupils who had become wives and mothers. From such, I learned the secret domestic history both of those I visited and of many of their intimate friends. And oh! what heartaches were the result of these years of quiet observation of the experience of my sex in domestic life. How many young hearts have revealed the fact, that what they had been trained to imagine the highest earthly felicity, was but the beginning of care, disappointment, and sorrow, and often led to the extremity of mental and physical suffering. Why was it that I was so often told that "young girls little imagined what was before them when they entered married life?" Why did I so often find those united to the most congenial and most devoted husbands expressing the hope that their daughters would never marry? For years these were my quiet, painful conjectures.

But the more I traveled, and the more I resided in health establishments, the more the conviction was pressed on my attention that there was a terrible decay of female health all over the land, and that this evil was bringing with it an incredible extent of individual, domestic, and social suffering, that was increasing in a most alarming ratio. At last, certain developments led me to take decided measures to obtain some reliable statistics on the subject. During my travels the last year I have sought all practicable methods of obtaining information, and finally adopted this course with most of the married ladies whom I met, either on my journeys or at the various health establishments at which I stopped.

I requested each lady first to write the *initials* of *ten* of the married ladies with whom she was best acquainted in her place of residence. Then she was requested to write at each name, her impressions as to the health of each lady. In this way, during the past year, I obtained statistics from about two hundred different places in almost all the Free States.

Before giving any of these, I will state some facts to show how far they are reliable: In the first place, the *standard of health* among American women is so low that few have a correct idea of *what a healthy woman is*. I have again and again been told by ladies that they were "perfectly healthy," who yet, on close inquiry, would allow that they were subject to frequent attacks of neuralgia, or to periodic nervous headaches, or to local ailments, to which they had become so accustomed, that they were counted as "nothing at all." A woman who has tolerable health finds herself so much above the great mass of her friends in this respect, that she feels herself a prodigy of good health.

In the next place, I have found that women who enjoy universal health are seldom well informed as to the infirmities of their friends. Repeatedly I have taken accounts from such persons, that seemed singularly favorable, when, on more particular inquiry, it was found that the greater part, who were set down as perfectly healthy women, were habitual sufferers from serious ailments. The delicate and infirm go for sympathy, not to the well and buoyant, but to those who have suffered like themselves.

This will account for some very favorable statements, given by certain ladies, that have not been inserted, because more accurate information showed their impressions to be false. As a general fact, it has been found that the more minute the inquiry, the greater the relative increase of ill health in all these investigations.

Again, I have found that ladies were predisposed usually to give the *most favorable* view of the case; for all persons like to feel that they are living in "a healthy place" rather than the reverse.

Again, I have found that almost every person in the result obtained, found that the case was worse than had been supposed, the proportion of sick or delicate to the strong and healthy being so small.

It must be remembered, that in regard to those marked as "sickly," "delicate," or "feeble," there can be no mistake, the knowledge being in all cases *positive*, while those marked as "well" may have ailments that are not known. For multitudes of American women, with their strict notions of propriety, and their patient and energetic spirit, often are performing every duty entirely silent as to any suffering or infirmities they may be enduring.

As to the terms used in these statements, in all cases there was a previous statement made as to the sense in which they were to be employed.

A "perfectly healthy" or "a vigorous and healthy woman" is one of whom there are *specimens* remaining in almost every place; such as used to *abound* when all worked, and *worked in pure air*.

Such a woman is one who can through the whole day be actively employed on her feet in all kinds of domestic duties without injury, and constantly and habitually has a feeling of perfect health and perfect freedom from pain. Not that she never has a fit of sickness, or takes a cold that interrupts the feeling of health, but that these are out of her ordinary experience.

A woman is marked "well" who usually has good health, but can not bear exposures, or long and great fatigue, without consequent illness.

A woman is marked "delicate" who, though she may be about and attend to most of her domestic employments, has a frail constitution that either has been undermined by ill health, or which easily and frequently yields to fatigue, or exposure, or excitement.

In the statements that follow, I shall place first those which are *most reliable,* inasmuch as in each case personal inquiries were made and the specific ailments were noted, to show that nothing was stated without full knowledge. As a matter of delicacy, the *initials* are changed, so that no individual can thus be identified.

MOST RELIABLE STATISTICS.

Milwaukee, Wis. Mrs. A. frequent sick headaches. Mrs. B. very feeble. Mrs. S. well, except chills. Mrs. L. poor health constantly. Mrs. D. subject to frequent headaches. Mrs. B. very poor health. Mrs. C. consumption. Mrs. A. pelvic displacements and weakness. Mrs. H. pelvic disorders and a cough. Mrs. B. always sick. Do not know one perfectly healthy woman in the place.

Essex, Vt. Mrs. S. very feeble. Mrs. D. slender and delicate. Mrs. S. feeble. Mrs. S. not well. Mrs. G. quite feeble. Mrs. C. quite feeble. Mrs. B. quite feeble. Mrs. S. quite slender. Mrs. B. quite feeble. Mrs. F. very feeble. Knows but one perfectly healthy woman in town.

Peru, N. Y. Mrs. C. not healthy. Mrs. H. not healthy. Mrs. E. healthy. Mrs. B. pretty well. Mrs. K. delicate. Mrs. B. not strong and healthy. Mrs. S. healthy and vigorous. Mrs. L. pretty well. Mrs. L. pretty well.

Canton, Penn. Mrs. R. feeble. Mrs. B. bad headaches. Mrs. D. bad headaches. Mrs. V. feeble. Mrs. S. erysipelas. Mrs. K. headaches, but tolerably well. Mrs. R. miserably sick and nervous. Mrs. G. poor health. Mrs. L. invalid. Mrs. C. invalid.

Oberlin, Ohio. Mrs. A. usually well, but subject to neuralgia. Mrs. D. poor health. Mrs. K. well, but subject to nervous headaches. Mrs. M. poor health. Mrs. C. not in good health. Mrs. P. not in good health. Mrs. P. delicate. Mrs. F. not in good health. Mrs. F. not in good health.

Wilmington, Del. Mrs. — —, scrofula. Mrs. B. in good health. Mrs. D. delicate. Mrs. H. delicate. Mrs. S. healthy. Mrs. P. healthy. Mrs. G. delicate. Mrs. O. delicate. Mrs. T. very delicate. Mrs.

S. headaches.

New Bedford, Mass. Mrs. B. pelvic diseases, and every way out of order. Mrs. J. W. pelvic disorders. Mrs. W. B. well, except in one respect. Mrs. C. sickly. Mrs. C. rather delicate. Mrs. P. not healthy. Mrs. C. unwell at times. Mrs. L. delicate. Mrs. B. subject to spasms. Mrs. H. very feeble. Can not think of but one perfectly healthy woman in the place.

Paxton, Vt. Mrs. T. diseased in liver and back. Mrs. H. stomach and back diseased. Mrs. W. sickly. Mrs. S. very delicate. Mrs. C. sick headaches, sickly. Mrs. W. bilious complaints. Mrs. T. very delicate. Mrs. T. liver complaint. Mrs. C. bilious sometimes, well most of the time. Do not know a perfectly healthy woman in the place. Many of these are the wives of wealthy farmers, who *overwork* when there is no need of it.

Crown Point, N. Y. Mrs. H. bronchitis. Mrs. K. very delicate. Mrs. A. very delicate. Mrs. A. diseased in back and stomach. Mrs. S. consumption. Mrs. A. dropsy. Mrs. M. delicate. Mrs. M. G. delicate. Mrs. P. delicate. Mrs. C. consumption. Do not know one perfectly healthy woman in the place.

Batavia, Illinois. Mrs. H. an invalid. Mrs. G. scrofula. Mrs. W. liver complaint. Mrs. K. pelvic disorders. Mrs. S. pelvic diseases. Mrs. B. pelvic diseases very badly. Mrs. B. not healthy. Mrs. T. very feeble. Mrs. G. cancer. Mrs. N. liver complaint. Do not know one healthy woman in the place.

Oneida, N. Y. Mrs. C. delicate. Mrs. P. scrofula. Mrs. S. not well. Mrs. L. very delicate and nervous. Mrs. L. invalid. Mrs. L. tolerably well. Mrs. A. invalid. Mrs. W. broken down. Mrs. D. feeble. Mrs. W. pale but pretty well.

North Adams, Mass. Mrs. R. scrofula and liver complaint. Mrs. R. consumption. Mrs. C. consumption. Mrs. B. liver complaint. Mrs. B. consumption. Mrs. B. general debility. Mrs. F. consumption. Mrs. W. paralytic. Mrs. W. confined always to her bed. Mrs. R. scrofula.

Charlotte, Vt. Mrs. W. spinal complaint. Mrs. D. spinal complaint. Mrs. N. spinal complaint. Mrs. R. bilious and paralytic. Mrs. R. pelvic disorders. Mrs. H. heart disease and dropsy. Mrs. B. dropsical. Mrs. H. pelvic disease and palsy. Mrs. H. scrofula and consumption. Mrs. S. quite delicate. Knows but one perfectly healthy woman in the place.

Maria, N. Y. Mrs. H. consumption. Mrs. E. dyspepsia. Mrs. T.

dyspepsia. Mrs. D. consumption. Mrs. P. dyspepsia. Mrs. R. sickly. Mrs. M. sickly. Mrs. R. delicate. Mrs. S. sickly. Mrs. R. consumption. Knows not one perfectly healthy woman in the place.

Vergennes, Vt. Mrs. L. delicate. Mrs. H. consumption. Mrs. H. consumption. Mrs. C. sickly. Mrs. S. liver complaint. Mrs. S. asthma. Mrs. S. sickly. Mrs. B. bronchitis. Mrs. S. consumptive. Mrs. B. delicate. Does not know a perfectly healthy woman in the place.

Brooklyn, N. Y. Mrs. B. very delicate. Mrs. G. scrofulous. Mrs. R. pelvic displacements. Mrs. I. nervous headaches. Mrs. A. pelvic diseases. Mrs. W. heart disease. Mrs. S. organic disease. Mrs. B. well but delicate. Mrs. L. well but delicate. Mrs. C. delicate.

Berlin, Conn. Mrs. A. dyspepsia. Mrs. B. quite delicate. Mrs. C. nervous headaches. Mrs. G. pelvic disorders. Mrs. M. weak lungs. Mrs. F. not sound. Mrs. C. delicate. Mrs. N. vigorous and healthy. Mrs. C. well. Mrs. A. delicate.

Whitestown, N. Y. Mrs. A. consumptive. Mrs. P. well but delicate. Mrs. M. well but delicate. Mrs. S. pelvic disorders. Mrs. R. dropsy. Mrs. B. pelvic disorders. Mrs. H. sick headaches. Mrs. K. organic disorder. Mrs. B. well but delicate. Mrs. T. bronchitis.

Proctorville, Vt. Mrs. B. well. Mrs. H. well. Mrs. S. pelvic and stomach disorders. Mrs. S. not healthy. Mrs. F. not healthy. Mrs. B. sickly. Mrs. C. not healthy. Mrs. W. not healthy. Mrs. A. vigorous and usually well. Knows no other strong and healthy woman.

Saratoga, N. Y. Mrs. M. pelvic disorders. Mrs. H. pelvic disorders. Mrs. A. pelvic disorders. Mrs. C. well. Mrs. C. neuralgia. Mrs. P. well. Mrs. T. consumptive. Mrs. J. tolerably well. Mrs. B. consumptive. Mrs. B. not well. Knows only one more well one among her acquaintance.

Saratoga, N. Y. (by another resident). Mrs. T. pelvic disorder. Mrs. C. pelvic disease. Mrs. H. not well. Mrs. S. well and strong. Mrs. B. tolerably well. Mrs. M. usually well. Mrs. O. headaches. Mrs. H. O. well. Mrs. S. delicate. Mrs. P. not well.

Canandaigua, N. Y. Mrs. A. well. Mrs. B. an invalid. Mrs. C. delicate. Mrs. H. delicate. Mrs. H. an invalid. Mrs. J. well. Mrs. P. delicate. Mrs. A. well. Mrs. C. an invalid. Mrs. W. well.

Livonia, N. Y. Mrs. H. rheumatic. Mrs. R. healthy and vigorous. Mrs. S. well. Mrs. R. good health. Mrs. P. very poor health. Mrs. B. well. Mrs. G. an invalid. Mrs. S. delicate. Mrs. T. poor health. Mrs. — —, pelvic disorders.

Turkhannock, Penn. Mrs. P. delicate and sickly. Mrs. L. delicate and well. Mrs. R. well and vigorous. Mrs. S. tolerably well. Mrs. C. well. Mrs. S. healthy. Mrs. T. consumption. Mrs. M. healthy. Mrs. R. well. Mrs. — —, pelvic disorders.

Bath, N. Y. Mrs. H. an invalid. Mrs. H. rheumatic. Mrs. H. healthy and vigorous. Mrs. S. vigorous. Mrs. K. delicate. Mrs. K. very healthy. Mrs. W. broken down. Mrs. W. tolerably well. Mrs. W. an invalid. Mrs. H. poor health.

Castleton, N. Y. Mrs. S. sickly. Mrs. W. healthy. Mrs. S. very delicate. Mrs. H. delicate. Mrs. H. delicate. Mrs. B. delicate. Mrs. W. not healthy. Mrs. H. not healthy. Mrs. D. not healthy.

The following were furnished by ladies who simply arranged the names of the ten married ladies best known to them in the place of their residence, in three classes, as marked over the several columns:

Residence.	Strong and perfectly Healthy.	Delicate or Diseased.	Habitual Invalids.
Hudson, Michigan	2	4	4
Castleton, Vermont	Not one.	9	1
Bridgeport, Vermont	4	4	2
Dorset, Vermont	Not one.	1	9
South Royalston, Mass.	4	2	4
Townsend, Vermont	4	3	3
Greenbush, New York	2	5	3
Southington, Connecticut	3	5	2
Newark, New Jersey	2	3	5
New York City	2	4	4
Oneida, New York	3	2	5
Milwaukee, Wisconsin	1	3	6
Rochester, New York	2	6	2
Plainfield, New Jersey	2	4	4
New York City	3	6	1
Lennox, Massachusetts	4	3	3

Union Vale, New York	2	5	3
Albany, New York	2	3	5
Hartford, Conn.	1	5	4
Cincinnati, Ohio	1	4	5
Andover, Mass.	2	5	3
Brunswick, Maine	2	5	3
Southington, Connecticut	3	5	2
Rochester, New York	2	6	2
Albany, New York	2	4	4
Milwaukee, Wisconsin	1	3	6
Plainfield, New Jersey	2	4	4
New York City	3	6	1
New York City	2	4	4
Worcester, Massachusetts	1	6	2
Newark, New Jersey	2	3	5
Bonhomme, Missouri	3	5	2
Painted Post, New York	1	3	6
Wilkins, New York	2	3	5
Johnsburg, New York	3	6	1
Burdett, New York	4	3	3
Horse Heads, New York	3	2	5
Pompey, New York	4	4	2
Tioga, Pennsylvania	3	4	3
Lodi, New York	2	5	3
Seymour, Connecticut	3	7	0
Williamsville, New York	4	2	4
Herkimer, New York	3	2	5
Hudson, Michigan	2	4	4
Kalamazoo, Michigan	3	6	1

The following are those not so reliable as the preceding, as the papers were some of them not clear, and some uncertainty about others for want of personal inquiry:

Cattskill, N. Y. Three vigorous, two well, three delicate, two sickly.

Batavia, N. Y. One vigorous, two well, three delicate, one sickly.

Ogden, N. Y. Three well, five well but delicate, two sickly.

Utica, N. Y. Nine well but not vigorous, one invalid.

Rhinebeck, N. Y. One vigorous, six well but not vigorous, one delicate, one invalid.

Cooperstown, N. Y. Two vigorous, five well, two delicate, two sickly.

Lima, N. Y. Five well, three delicate, two sickly.

Rockaway, N. Y. Two vigorous, five well, one delicate, two sickly.

Brockport, N. Y. Three vigorous, six well, one delicate, one sickly.

Buffalo, N. Y. Five well, five delicate.

Potsdam, N. Y. Eight tolerably well, two sickly.

Rome, N. Y. Two well, seven tolerably well, one sickly.

Rochester, N. Y. Four well, three delicate, three sickly.

Princeton, N. J. Four well, five well but delicate, three sickly.

Muncy, Penn. Two vigorous, six well but delicate, two sickly.

The remainder of accounts furnished being less reliable, for want of opportunities of definite inquiry on my part, and will therefore be omitted. But they do not essentially differ from these presented.

I will now add my own personal observation. First, in my own family connection: I have nine married sisters and sisters-in-law, all of them either delicate or invalids, except two. I have fourteen married female cousins, and not one of them but is either delicate, often ailing, or an invalid. In my wide circle of friends and acquaintance all over the land out of my family circle, the same impression is made. In Boston I can not remember but one married female friend who is perfectly healthy. In Hartford, Conn., I can think of only one. In New Haven, but one. In Brooklyn, N. Y., but one. In New York city, but one. In Cincinnati, but one. In Buffalo, Cleveland, Chicago, Milwaukee, Detroit, those whom I have visited are either delicate or invalids. I am not able to recall, in my immense circle of friends and acquaintance all over the Union, so many as *ten* married ladies born in this century and country, who are perfectly sound, healthy, and vigorous. Not that I believe there are not more than this among the friends with whom I have associated, but among all whom I can bring to mind of whose health I have any accurate knowledge, I can not find this number of entirely sound and healthy women.

Another thing has greatly added to the impression of my own observations, and that is the manner in which my inquiries have been met. In a majority of cases, when I have asked for the number of perfectly healthy women in a given place, the first impulsive answer has been "not one." In other cases, when the reply has been more favorable, and I have asked for specifics, the result has always been such as to diminish the number calculated, rather than to increase it. With a few exceptions the persons I have asked, who had not directed their thoughts to the subject, and took a favorable view of it, have expressed surprise at the painful result obtained in their own immediate circle.

But the thing which has pained and surprised me the most is the result of inquiries among the country-towns and industrial classes in our country. I had supposed that there would be a great contrast between the statements gained from persons from such places, and those furnished from the wealthy circles, and especially from cities. But such has not been the case. It will be seen that the larger portion of the accounts inserted in the preceding pages are from country-towns, while a large portion of the worst accounts were taken from the industrial classes.

As another index of the state of health among the industrial classes may be mentioned these facts: During the past year I made my usual inquiry of the wife of a Methodist clergyman, who resided in a small country-town in New York. Her reply was, "There are no healthy women where I live, and my husband says he would travel a great many miles for the pleasure of finding one."

In another case I conversed with a Baptist clergyman and his wife, in Ohio, and their united testimony gave this result in three places where his parishioners were chiefly of the industrial class. They selected at random ten families best known in each place:

Worcester, Ohio. Women in perfect health, two. In medium health, one. *Invalids, seven.*

Norwalk, Ohio. Women perfectly healthy, one, but doubtfully so. Medium, none. *Invalids, nine.*

Cleveland, Ohio. Women in perfect health, one. Medium health, two. *Invalids, seven.*

In traveling at the West the past winter, I repeatedly conversed with drivers and others among the laboring class on this subject, and always heard such remarks as these: "Well! it is strange how sickly the women are getting!" "Our women-folks don't have such health as they used to do!"

One case was very striking. An old lady from New England told me her mother had twelve children; eleven grew up healthy, and raised families. Her father's mother had fifteen children, and raised them all; and all but one, who was drowned, lived to a good old age. This lady stated that she could not remember that there was a single "weakly woman" in the town where she lived when she was young.

This lady had two daughters with her, both either delicate or diseased, and a sick niece from that same town, once so healthy when the old lady was young. This niece told me she could not think of even one really robust, strong, and perfectly healthy woman in that place! The husband of this old lady told me that in his youth he also did not know of any sickly women in the place where he was reared.

A similar account was given me by two ladies, residents of Goshen, Litchfield Co., Connecticut.

The elder lady gave the following account of her married acquaintance some forty years ago in that place:

> Mrs. L. strong and perfectly healthy. Mrs. A. healthy and strong as a horse. Mrs. N. perfectly well always. Mrs. H. strong and well. Mrs. B. strong and generally healthy, but sometimes ailing a little. Mrs. R. always well. Mrs. W. strong and well. Mrs. G. strong and hearty. Mrs. H. strong and healthy. Mrs. L. strong and healthy.

All the above persons performed their own family work.

The following account was given by the daughter of the lady mentioned above, and the list is chiefly made up of daughters of the above healthy women living at this time in the same town:

> Mrs. C. constitution broken by pelvic disorders. Mrs. P. very delicate. Mrs. L. delicate and feeble. Mrs. R. feeble and nervous. Mrs. S. bad scrofulous humors. Mrs. D. very feeble, head disordered. Mrs. R. delicate and sickly. Mrs. G. healthy. Mrs. D. healthy. Mrs. W. well.

These last three were the only healthy married women she knew in the place.

I have received statements from more than a hundred other places besides those recorded here. The larger portion of these were taken by others, or else by myself in such circumstances that I could not make the inquiries needed to render them reliable, and some I have lost. The general impression made, even by these alone, would bring out very nearly the same result. The proportion of the sick and delicate to those who were strong and well was, in the majority of cases, a melancholy story. But among them were a few cases in which a very favorable statement was verified by close examination. In several such cases, however, most of the healthy women proved to be either English, Irish, or Scotch. In one case, a lady from a country-town, not far from Philadelphia, gave an account, showing eight out of ten perfectly healthy, and the other two were not very much out of health. On inquiry, I found that this was a Quaker settlement, and most of the healthy ones were Quakers.

In one town of Massachusetts, the lady giving the information said all the ten she gave were healthy, but two. Her associates were all women who were in easy circumstances, and did their own family work. These two places, however, are the *only* instances I have found, where, on close inquiry, the majority was on the side of good health.

There is no doubt that there are many places like these two, of which some resident would report that a majority of their acquaintance were healthy women; but out of about two hundred towns and cities, located in most of the Free States, only two have as yet presented so favorable a case in the line of my inquiries during the year in which they have been prosecuted.

Let these considerations now be taken into account. The generation represented in these statistics, by universal consent, is a feebler one than that which immediately preceded. Knowing the changes in habits of living, in habits of activity, and in respect to *pure air*, we properly infer that it must be so, while universal testimony corroborates the inference.

The present generation of parents, then, have given their children, so far as the mother has hereditary influence, feebler constitutions than the former generation received, so that most of our young girls have started in life with a more delicate organization than their mothers. Add to this the sad picture given in a former letter of all the abuses of health suffered by the young during their early education, and what are the present prospects of the young women who are now entering married life?

This view of the case, in connection with some dreadful developments which will soon be indicated, proved so oppressive and exciting that it has been too painful and exhausting to attempt any investigation as to the state of health among young girls. But every where I go, mothers are constantly saying, "What shall I do? As soon as my little girl begins school she has the headache." Or this—"I sent my daughter to such a boarding-school, but had to take her away on account of her health."

The public schools of our towns and cities, where the great mass of the people are to be educated, are the special subject of remark and complaint in this respect.

Consider also that "man that is born of a woman" depends on her not only for the constitutional stamina with which he starts in life, but for all he receives during the developments of infancy and the training of childhood, and what are we to infer of the condition and prospects of the other sex now in the period of education?

Printed by Libri Plureos GmbH in Hamburg,
Germany

9 789361 384653